*L*ove is the Hardest Lesson

Margaret Hope
and Allen Bacon

June 28, 1942

Margaret Hope
and Allen Bacon

June 27, 1993

*L*ove is the Hardest Lesson

A Memoir

Margaret Hope Bacon

Pendle Hill Publications

For information, please address Pendle Hill Publications
338 Plush Mill Road
Wallingford, Pennsylvania 19086-6099
1-800-742-3150

Library of Congress Cataloging-in-Publication Data

Bacon, Margaret Hope
    Love is the Hardest Lesson: A Memoir/Margaret H. Bacon
    p. cm.
    ISBN 0-87574-936-4
    1. Bacon, Margaret Hope. 2. Springfield State Hospital of the
State of Maryland (Sykesville, Md.)--Biography. 3. Pacifists--United
States--Biography. 4. Quakers--United States--Biography. 5. Psychiat-
ric aides--Maryland--Biography. 6. Psychiatric hospitals--Sociological
aspects. 7. World War, 1939-1945--Conscientious objectors--United
States. I Title.
    RC439 .B22 1999
    362.2'1'092--dc21
    [B]

                                                        99-045314

Love is the hardest lesson in Christianity,
but for that reason it should be
most our care to learn it.

—William Penn

For Allen

Foreword

$\mathcal{M}$y experiences as the wife of a conscientious objector to World War II have continued to haunt me throughout a life time. I worked in a state mental hospital. For a long while I felt I could not write about the personal crises we experienced at Sykesville without hurting living people. I therefore turned my account into short stories, none of which I submitted for publication. Instead, I created a file, at which I would periodically look and sigh.

More than twenty years ago, I decided to try to string these stories into a novel. This got a good deal of favorable response, but the only publisher who wanted to bring it out asked that I rewrite it as a first person factual account. This I was unwilling to do at the time, so the novel joined the stories in the ever growing file.

But the memories of Sykesville and what I learned there would not go away, and I began to feel that for the sake of my children, and the many other young people who feel to me like my spiritual heirs, I must write the book. Many of the people described are now dead; others surely have mellowed in their recollections. I have carefully changed the names of all but a very few of the participants. And I have slightly rearranged the order of some of the events, both to protect the privacy of others, and also to compress the story into a reasonable space.

Working from my fictionalized accounts of this period, I cannot now be sure which details I remember as they happened and which I have embellished over time. For records I have only a series of letters which we wrote home to my husband's mother at the time, plus the memories of the few friends with whom we have kept in touch. Although I am a historian, I have not gone back to consult other records for the sake of accuracy. This seems to me more important as the account of one woman's reaction to her times than as an objective account of those times.

Much of what I have written seems very naive to me now; a very young woman's struggle with some profound issues. I hardly recognize myself. It was tempting to modify some of these early judgments in light of experience. I have tried, however, to avoid that temptation so that the manuscript can reflect as accurately as possible the mood of that time.

This is the story of an effort to understand and apply the principles of nonviolence to the day-to-day life of a state mental hospital, our successes and our failures, and what we learned about the relationship of nonviolence to our deepest selves. For me it was an exploration of the spiritual basis from which nonviolence must spring, and the power of love to reach through incredible barriers and teach its lessons to the human heart.

Chapter I

*F*OR YEARS I CONTINUED TO DREAM that I was back in Sykesville. In the dream I am hurrying down one of the wards, past the dark tiled walls. A shapeless woman is polishing the waxed floor, walking monotonously back and forth. I smell the same old smell of human waste and strong chemicals; hear the same incoherent shouts from the locked wards. I am eager to reach the heavy doors at the end of the ward and escape to safety beyond, and one hand reaches for the keys I wear at my belt, to make sure they are really there.

But now I see that a group of patients are standing between me and the door, and I grow afraid that they are going to confront me. They are wearing the same shapeless gray gowns as always, and I see the pallor of their faces, their slack mouths, and vacant eyes. One detaches herself from the group and comes for me, and I experience the same terror that I felt that first day at Sykesville. Is the patient Agnes Holler?

I awakened always from this dream with my heart pounding. Then I grew slowly calmer and began to remember Agnes and all that she taught me about fear, and the power of love to overcome terror and violence.

Sykesville was the common name for Springfield State Hospital, a mental hospital located in the village of Sykesville, Maryland, west of Baltimore. During World War II my husband, Allen, was assigned there as a conscientious objector to war. Although a Quaker, he had chosen to go to a camp run by the Brethren Service in northern Michigan when he was drafted in August of 1943. From there he was transferred to Sykesville. I was living in New York City at the time, and we wanted to be nearer one another.

Because of the chronic shortage of personnel during wartime, attendants were badly needed for the wards. So were nurses, social workers, secretaries, and dietitians. Many wives of conscientious objectors therefore were able to find jobs in the mental hospitals in order to be with their husbands. I was considering this step when I first visited Sykesville.

I arrived on a dark, wet winter day. The hospital looked neat and trim, set in the midst of a large, isolated landscape on a well-kept 1600-acre tract in the rolling Maryland countryside. The architecture was nondescript Georgian institutional style. It might have been a college except for the heavily barred windows. Inside, the walls were tiled halfway up with dark ceramic tiles, the floors were covered with highly waxed and polished linoleum, and the ceilings painted a dark buff. Even in the Main admission wing, where a few curtains were hung, the atmosphere was dreary; elsewhere it was abysmally depressing.

The institution consisted of four groups of large brick buildings placed apart from each other. There was the Men's group at one end of the grounds, and the Women's group at the other, housing chronic patients. There was the central Hubner Group where new patients were admitted and treated, and where all serious medical needs were attended. One set of buildings comprising Hubner was the tuberculosis ward. TB was still rampant in these pre-penicillin days, and many chronic patients came down with it in the Men's Group or the Women's Group, and were transferred to Hubner for treatment. Hubner also contained the hospital administration, the social service department, the recreational therapy wing, a small operating room, and the morgue. A fourth set of buildings, the Epileptic Colony, housed epileptics whose seizures could not be sufficiently controlled so that they could live outside the hospital. It also had housing for married ward attendants.

Life in a mental hospital was a far different experience in 1944 than in 1999. Tranquilizers had not come into use, and the heavily drugged but quiet patient whom one now encounters was unknown. Instead many of the disturbed patients roamed about the halls of their wards, hallucinating and shouting, and often fighting back when the attendants tried to control them. Strait jackets and locked wards were used for the most obstreperous, and the only treatment available was hydrotherapy or the new electric shock or insulin therapies, both reserved for the patients who had entered the hospital most recently, and were regarded as having the best chance of recovery. Unless patients spontaneously got better, they often ended up spending years, even a lifetime, in the hospital. Overcrowding was therefore a serious problem, and led to further uproar on the wards, as highly disturbed patients were jammed together into small spaces. Attendants on these wards had to be constantly alert to personal danger, and to preventing patients from harming one another. A popular book of the era, based on one woman's experience of a state mental hospital was accurately titled: *The Snake Pit.*

When Allen first arrived at Sykesville he was assigned to Men's Group, "shit castle" as it was familiarly called. Here the older and often incontinent patients passed their dreary days with no treatment, no change in their routine from day to day, week to week, month to month, year to year. Two doctors presided over the whole of Men's Group, some 1100 patients. Like most doctors who stayed in state hospitals for a long period of time, they had both given up doing more than the bare minimum required by law. Though they made occasional rounds, they paid little attention to individual patients, and it was hard for the attendants to persuade them to come and see sick patients, or even those who were dying. In fact, once while Allen was working in the Group, a patient died and remained in his bed for several days before a doctor could be persuaded to see him and sign the necessary papers so that he could be taken to the morgue. With the smells already rampant on the ward, the smell of decaying flesh didn't really make that much difference, Allen said.

The first time I visited Sykesville, Allen took me with him up to the Men's Group where he ran an errand. I had planned to wait for him in the reception area, but one of the doctors happened to be passing through, and offered to show me the wards. Although the first ward he took me on was supposed to be a quiet one, I was terrified by the jabbering, gesticulating men all about me, and clung close to my guide. Not close enough however, to prevent one large, strong-looking patient from creeping across the floor toward me, and taking off my shoes. I was terrified, but when I managed to get the doctor's attention he simply waved the patient away and went on talking to me as though nothing had happened. Clearly it was possible to become habituated to what I regarded as sheer bedlam. As for me, I could hardly wait to get away from the place, and I promised myself I would never return.

And yet, three months later, I joined Allen at Sykesville. Our separation was putting strains on our very new marriage; it seemed clear that we needed to be together if it were to thrive. Despite my dread it was time to fulfill my side of the bargain. With Allen's encouragement I applied for a job on the wards, with the understanding that in three months I would be transferred to a higher paid and more pleasant job in the social service department. We were assigned a room on the third floor of the married attendants quarters in the Epileptic colony. The room was a small, dark, airless and dreary box which we fixed up as best we could with a lamp, a bedspread, a rug, and Van Gogh reproductions on the wall.

The first day after I arrived, I went to see about my ward assignment. Allen had already learned that I was to be placed at first on the female tubercular ward of the Hubner group. Other attendants regarded this assignment as an easy job. The TB patients were generally too old and too feeble to offer much fight, and the work of the ward attendants was more involved with nursing than with trying to restrain disturbed patients. There was some risk of catching the disease, but I was assured that by means of x-raying the attendants regularly, requiring everyone to wear a mask, and a routine of constant hand-washing, this risk could be minimized.

If this were not good fortune enough, Allen himself had been transferred from the Men's Group to the violent admission ward, South IA, in the Hubner group so that we could work and eat our meals in the same buildings. The head of the social service unit, we learned, had helped to arrange this for us. Matilda van Dusen, as I will call her, had interviewed me for the job I was to have later, and had liked me. I knew nothing about social work, but I was a writer and Matilda was interested in having some of her ideas in social work interpreted.

Mrs. Dixon, the charge attendant for the Hubner Admissions Group, was a kind, motherly woman who seemed touched by my youth (I was 22) and my air of timidity. She gave me a uniform, made sure that I knew how to take a temperature, make a bed, and empty a bedpan, and took me to the ward to introduce me to my future colleagues. I met Miss Becker, a short, frank, manly sort of woman with closely cropped black hair and a chin blue from shaving, and Emma Blossom, a younger rather blowzy woman with big blue eyes. They greeted me pleasantly enough, and the ward seemed quiet in mid afternoon except for an occasional hollow cough. I returned to Allen feeling that it was not going to be nearly as bad as I had expected.

At supper that night we sat in the staff dining room with several older, more experienced c.o. couples. They were all eager to hear about my placement, and all ready to congratulate me on a soft berth. It went to show how much things had changed recently, they said. In the early days of the Unit, the c.o.'s were despised by patients, attendants, and administration alike. The attendants in particular saw these college kids, too yellow to go to war, as a threat. We came, took over jobs which the attendants had held all their lives, and claimed that by doing so they were making a comparable sacrifice to going overseas to fight. Doing work of national importance, as the Selective Service Act read. But when the war ended we would go back to college, or to our white collar careers, and the attendants would go on doing the dirty work, which was the only work they knew. This source of bitterness, combined with outraged patriotism, produced an ugly hostility. Many of the female attendants had husbands or sons in the service, and regarded it as an act of loyalty to these far-away loved ones to hate the c.o.'s. In the early days of the unit, the attendants sometimes persuaded violently disturbed patients that it was the c.o.'s who were responsible for their troubles. Or walked away when the c.o.'s or the c.o. wives were in trouble with hard-to-control patients. Or simply left all the hardest and dirtiest work of the ward to the despised conchies.

But now, the old-timers assured us happily, things were very different. The mood had changed; the administration was beginning to realize that it could not run the hospital now without the c.o.'s and to act accordingly. Some of the most bitter troublemakers among the old-time attendants had left; the rest had lapsed into sullen hostility. C.o.'s were given more and more of the responsible jobs, and their wives were hired as nurses and social workers. One of the younger psychiatrists had even developed friendships with members of the unit. Clearly Allen and I were being given the red carpet treatment. We ought to be duly grateful. We should have been around two years ago.

We spent a few hours after supper in the room of another unit couple, listening to music, then went early to bed. I wanted to get a good night's sleep before my first day on the ward. We all worked from six a.m. to seven thirty p.m. with one half hour out for each meal and two hours "off" sometimes in the course of the afternoon. Since this meant being on one's feet for ten hours, it was necessary to get plenty of rest, as well as to wear sturdy shoes to work.

It was, I remember, a night of full moon. Allen was soon asleep, but I lay awake and watched a path of moonlight as it first stole in our window, made a beam across the floor, climbed the opposite wall, moved across it slowly, fell back on the floor, and slipped away again at the window. Fear is too specific a word for the numbing terror I fought all night, never being able to tell myself what I dreaded, nor guessing that the enemy might be within. One hundred times I reminded myself how friendly Miss Becker had seemed, how welcoming Emma, how quiet the ward. There would be TB germs, sure, but I would wear a mask. And just think, in three short months I would escape from the ward into the quiet and order and civility of the social service department. Hadn't I heard from our friends the night before how much better the atmosphere was now? How kindly disposed the officials were toward us?

All in vain. This sort of reassurance had nothing to do with the feelings I had, nor was it able to make the slightest dent in my awful suspicion that I had trapped myself into a situation from which there was no escape. In my panic I thought of flight in the only way I had known as a child, when I did not want to go to school. Was I becoming ill? Was my head aching? Stomach churning? Did I have a slight sore throat? But no, even if I were sick for a few days it would not postpone the moment when I had to enter that ward.

I must have dozed a bit toward the end of the night, for all too soon the alarm was ringing and we were on our feet, fumbling for our clothes in the dim light of dawn. Allen looked like young Dr. Kildare in his whites, whereas my uniform had a way of bunching around my middle and making me appear short and fat. After the sleepless night my bones felt hollowed out, and there was sand under my eyelids. No matter, it was important now simply to get out of the room which imprisoned so many terrors of the night and be on our way to the 6 a.m. breakfast.

It was a beautiful morning in early April, with dew sparkling on the grass, and birds singing. Outside I immediately felt a little better, and walking across the grounds we held hands. Breakfast in the attendant's dining room at Hubner was always the same--greasy eggs, greasy bacon, greasy toast, lumpy cereal, bitter coffee-but at least there was a lot of everything, and after a winter of living on wartime rations and a tiny budget the sheer amount of the food seemed lavish to me. As a child of the Depression I always felt I ought to eat whatever was available. This morning I ate more than I thought I would, managed a parting smile to Allen and showed up at my ward a few minutes early.

"O, so you're here," Miss Becker said. She showed me the little attendants room where I could leave my things, then took me to the nursing station and pointed out the patients' charts on which I was to mark their temperatures. Since few of the patients could be trusted with a thermometer in their mouths, all temperatures were to be taken rectally. Miss Becker helped me with the first few, then, seeing that I could manage, went off to take care of other matters. It was an unpleasant job; the old women did not like it, and cursed at me and resisted me, and several had involuntary bowel movements I had to clean up, but I had had a similar nursing experience and knew how to hold my breath to avoid nausea.

While I was in high school I had worked one summer for a neighbor of my grandmother's in Tampa, Florida. Mrs. Frazier had crippling arthritis, and needed me, she said, as her amanuensis to keep up with her extensive correspondence. If I would write letters at her dictation, she would pay me $5 a week. In fact, although I wrote many letters, I also gave Mrs. Frazier her bath, prepared and served her meals, and emptied her bedpan, which she loaded copiously due to some medicine she took. Her bedroom was hot and airless, and the odors multiplied, despite my best efforts.

I hated the job, less because of its physical than its mental unpleasantness. Mrs. Frazier was a Colonial Dame, a Daughter of the Barons of Runnymede, and Daughter of the Confederacy, and an anti-Semite. Since my grandmother happened to be Jewish, one would think she would have modified her stringent attitudes in her dictation to me, but this was not the case. My grandparents were among the first settlers of Tampa and were therefore good Jews, and not to be confused with the rest. She even lent my grandmother a virulently anti-Semitic book, "the Protocols of Zion" purporting to be a plot by the Jews to take over the world. From Mrs. Frazier's point of view Father Coughlin was on the right track. It was very hard to write down some of the things she wanted said in her letters. At times emptying the bedpan was a relief. Well, at least she had prepared me for Sykesville.

I completed the round of temperature taking without incident and began feeding bed patients their breakfasts. After this it was time to fetch bedpans and change sheets, and give bed patients their baths, while the charge attendant gave out medicine and fresh sputum cups. After the long night of terror, the work seemed easy, and my spirits began to soar. Trotting down the hall, a bedpan in each hand I found myself singing a folk song I had learned in New York that winter with the apt refrain "swiftly flowing water."

It was toward the end of the morning that Miss Becker looked up, and seeing me pause momentarily, remarked that if I had nothing better to do I could give Agnes Holler a bath. Since all the patients were one blur to me, I had no idea who Agnes Holler was. Miss Becker solved the mystery by indicating a locked door at the end of a short corridor adjacent to the nursing station. "Watch out when you open the door that she doesn't get away from you," she cautioned.

I took the key she proffered, walked down the hall and peered into a small window of thick glass, reinforced with metal wiring. The cell into which I looked was sunlit, tiled, and perfectly empty except for a creature which huddled against the wall. It was a young woman, I saw, tall and rather well built, but painfully thin, with wild black hair and distraught features. She was totally naked, and her body was dabbed with yellow feces.

I looked back at the nursing station. Miss Becker and Emma were watching me, smiling. It was not a friendly smile. I caught a sudden vision of myself as I might seem to them, prissy, polite, pretending that I found their work--their lifelong work-something I could pick up in a morning. Go ahead, they were thinking, go ahead and let's see what your college education does for you now.

I remembered then that one of the experienced unit wives had warned me. "There's one patient over there to look out for. Agnes Holler, She's got tuberculosis of the bowels and she is as bad as anyone on South Two A. [The violent women's ward] Don't let them stick you with her." But I had been stuck, and there appeared to be no turning back. I took a deep breath and put the key in the lock.

"Come Agnes, I am going to give you a bath," I said as quietly as I could.

Agnes remained in her corner oblivious, mumbling. It sounded like some sort of shopping list she recited, although only occasionally would I catch a scrap of it. ". . . and little yellow place mats, and yellow bath mats, and little lilac tea towels."

"Come, Agnes," I repeated.

For a moment she continued to mutter. Then suddenly she came toward me, arms upraised, and I saw she meant to strike me.

Senior lifesaving drill came to my aid. I caught one raised arm by the wrist, pulled her across me, and pinned her arm to her back. I was now behind her, and though the smell was more than I thought I could bear I held on tight while she struggled against me. She was strong, but sick; I could feel the heat of her fever and the sharpness of her bones through the thin flesh of her arms. Pity replaced my fear, and I relaxed my grip a bit. "Come Agnes, I am going to give you a bath," I repeated again.

Holding her still in front of me, but more loosely, I led her to the bathroom, turned on the water with my free hand, and guided her into the large old fashioned bath tub. As the tub began to fill with warm water she relaxed, and her mumbling resumed. ". . . and little yellow place mats and little violet bath mats." Perhaps she was planning a bridal trousseau. I was no longer there. In fact, I had never been there, except for that one moment when she lunged. Knowing this, my fear subsided still further. I was eager to get her safely back to her cell, but I took time to get her clean, and even talked to her a little as I scrubbed.

"How are you getting on with Agnes?" Miss Becker asked from the door way.

"Just fine," I said, busy with my washcloth.

"Keep your eye on her," Miss Becker said, uneasily. "She's apt to jump out of the tub at any moment."

"I'll be careful," I promised. I could see that she was surprised; at how docile Agnes seemed, and how collected I appeared. Surprised and perhaps disappointed. I felt a glow of pride. After she left I helped Agnes out of the bath and dried her carefully with a large white towel and put a clean robe on her. I even tried to comb the matted hair, but Agnes jerked away roughly.

"All right," I told her, "but someday I'll comb it, and I won't hurt you."

I took her back to her cell then, and locked her up, and spent the rest of the day scurrying around, trying to keep up with Miss Becker's orders. It was clear that I was going to get the most work and the dirtiest jobs on the ward. But then, I was the new girl. I was young and strong and I did not mind so much. I had faced the very worst at the beginning, and somehow I had managed. The long sleepless night I had spent watching the moonlight sweep across the room now seemed far removed, unreal. I was tired but I was triumphant. It was just a job, and I could do it, as I had done other jobs before.

I could hardly wait to get off duty and tell Allen about my triumph. He was duly appreciative, but midway through my recital it occurred to me that he had faced and dealt with many similar situations in the four months he had already spent at Sykesville. What I had done was routine. Still, I was vastly relieved that I could do it, and slept long and soundly that night.

From that day on, Agnes was my special charge. Everyone began to notice that she was more docile and tranquil with me than with the other attendants. I was therefore the one to bathe and feed her, to take her to X ray, to try to take her temperature. I cleaned out her cell, and combed her hair, and even once cleaned her fingernails.

Not that I affected some great change in Agnes. She grew, if anything, worse during the period I worked on TB II. Her mumblings were more rapid and abstract, back in her cell she inevitably tore off her clothes and threw her food and smeared herself. At night, and on my days off, she was reportedly the same old hellcat, attacking the attendants when given the least opportunity.

Even though she seemed different with me, she never gave the slightest sign of knowing I was there. I talked to her as I bathed and fed her, but there was never any indication that she heard a word I said. The nurses told me it was years since she had spoken a word beyond her incessant mumble. I think the other attendants thought I was crazy to chatter away to her, but I was lonely on the ward where no one spoke to me except to give orders, and talking to Agnes helped to pass the time.

Besides, in a curious way, I became fond of Agnes. She was the Everest I had climbed, the clay I had potted, the lion I had tamed. I was never completely without fear of her, but I felt close, closer than with many of the other patients I subsequently knew. And as fear waned there became room--as there usually does-- for affection. I had a warm feeling for Agnes, and being with her became the bright spot of my day. Off the ward, I thought about her a great deal. What could have started the retreat that had resulted in her hopeless state of deterioration? Could it really be some childhood hurt too bad to face? Or could only a chemical change account for this transformation of woman into creature? For she seemed at times no more than an animal, and I felt sure that whatever scrap of intelligence, whatever touch of soul, whatever capacity to love she had once possessed had been drowned years ago.

After a while, my days on the ward improved still further. Miss Becker and Emma continued to keep me at a distance until one morning when I walked into the attendants room and found them embracing. Then later that day they took me into their confidence. They were lovers, and persecuted for it by the hospital administrators. Since I was a social outcast too, a conchie's wife, I could understand their bitter feelings toward the other attendants.

The chief tormentor of the c.o.'s and their wives was a woman called Mrs. Clement. Mrs. Clement had a husband in the army (who upon discharge never returned to her, we were later told) and she felt that loyalty to him and patriotism demanded her shouting "you yellow bellies" at us several times a day. Mrs. Clement was also outraged by the Becker-Emma relationship, and chided Miss Becker about being seen holding hands with Emma. Becker told me about this, and I sympathized with her, and from then on things were a little easier.

After several weeks I experienced my first night duty on TB II. I was alone all night, except for an attendant who came to relieve me at midnight so I could have my supper of greasy cold cuts and bitter coffee in the attendants' dining room. In the nursing station, a hexagonal structure at the intersection of two wings of the ward, I sat in a small island of light with darkness lapping at its shore all around. It was spooky. In the light was normalcy; beyond in the darkness, the odd mutterings and coughings of patients, and whatever else imagination could conjure up. I heard the coughs--deep coughs, syrupy coughs, dry coughs, high coughs--but I also heard other things, stealthy footsteps, weird chucklings. It was an actual relief to leave the island of light and with my flashlight in my hand to penetrate the encircling darkness. I would have to make such forays when it was time to take the temperature of an aging patient whose fever had been up all day, or to change a sputum cup of a constant cougher, or investigate a patient whose mutterings were growing louder, and might need another dose of Paraldahyde, our only form of sleeping medicine. At least such trips laid to rest the imaginary ghosts I had conjured up. But I had to be careful not to disturb other patients, and stir up extra trouble for myself. I was always glad to return to the safety of the nursing station.

The hours seemed to stretch on and on, endlessly. There were a few charts to keep, a few temperatures to take in the course of the night, but most of the patients slept heavily from dusk to dawn, thanks to the heavy doses of Paraldehyde we gave each one of them, and the problem for the attendant was mainly to keep alert, and keep sufficiently occupied to fight down fear. I wrote letters, I read, I sometimes tried to write poetry, but there was an undercurrent of constant watchfulness that made it hard to lose oneself in such pursuits.

Eventually, the very dimmest of light would appear, shadow forms would begin to detach themselves from the general darkness, the lapping waves would recede, and dawn come.

After the nights on duty, the days seemed easier. It was twelve hours of hard work, and one needed a strong stomach, but I had learned to do it. The hours passed in a soothing routine-- temperatures, breakfast, baths, ward clean-up, doctors rounds, patients to x-ray, temperatures, lunch, rest hours, medicines, temperatures, supper bedtime. Occasionally some patient had a visitor, or was well enough to go to occupational therapy or out for a walk, but most of them never left the ward and we stayed with them all day, taking time only for our own meals and our hour off. Patients and attendants, we were locked together in a curious communion with a rhythm of its own.

I did not stay long on the TB ward. After six weeks the doctors took a patch test on my back and it came out negative. This meant that I had no TB anti-bodies; the price of a protected childhood, and was therefore a prime target to catch the disease. I must be moved immediately to another ward. I did not want to get sick, but in a way I was sorry. I had come to feel comfortable with Miss Becker and Emma. They were the first lesbian couple I had known, and I think they helped to knock out of me whatever latent homophobia I possessed. I was familiar with the ward routine, and I knew most of the patients.

But most of all, I found I was reluctant to leave Agnes. On my last day on the ward I gave her an extra long bath and I realized that I was going to miss her in a funny way. I told her I was leaving but would return to visit, and I said good-bye, but of course she did not respond.

Chapter II

*T*he road which brought me to the door of Agnes Holler's cell in March of 1943 was a long one. People sometimes assumed that because I was married to a Quaker I must also have come from a Quaker background. Nothing could be further from the case. I was born and brought up in New York City, the only child of an artist from the South, and a nurse from Canada. My father's family was originally a German Jewish one; but they had come to the American South in the 1840s, and, scattered in small towns in Georgia and Florida, had eventually lost their Jewish identity. My grandparents were Christian Scientists; my father often sang in an Episcopal choir. He was rather conflicted about his Jewish background, and told few people about it while I was growing up. In fact, I am not sure I knew until I was about thirteen.

My mother's people had emigrated to Canada from Scotland and from Ireland at the beginning of the nineteenth century, but living in isolated villages had kept their patterns of speech and culture. My maternal grandmother, whom I never knew, still had something of an Irish accent. The Grants were humble and simple people; though Anglican they lived in the South of Ireland. The Hopes from Scotland were Presbyterian. My mother grew up going to a local Congregational church.

My parents might never have met had it not been for World War I. My father, having recently graduated from the Chicago Art Institute and set himself up in New York City as a free lance artist, wanted to join the air force. Turned down by the Americans because of flat feet, he enrolled in the Canadian Royal Air Force, was trained in Texas, and became so expert he was chosen as an instructor. He was assigned to France, to teach techniques to pilots behind the lines. On his last flight in Texas he crashed, and was so seriously injured that his life was regarded as in danger. The joy stick of the plane had plowed a furrow through his lips and nose, but his face was simply slapped together roughly while the medical staff concentrated on setting his broken bones and draining a deep and dangerous chest wound. When he was well enough to be moved he was sent to the military ward of Toronto General Hospital, where my mother was the charge nurse.

My mother had sparkling blue eyes, pink cheeks, and auburn hair. She was kind and efficient, and she loved to laugh. As soon as he was well enough, my father drew cartoons of all the other inmates of the military ward, and poked gentle fun at some of the doctors and nurses. Mother was highly amused, and did not seem to think that my father's botched up face looked funny. She had had a dictatorial father and responded to my father's perpetual gentleness. To my father, I think, she represented all the things he had wished to be, growing up as a minority in a Southern town. They fell in love, were married in May of 1919 and moved to New York City where my father could practice his calling as a free lance artist and where, they both assumed, mother would fit right in to my father's circle of artist friends.

Of course she didn't. A deeply shy and sometimes conventional person, I think she was a little shocked by outspoken women in my father's previous circle. Instead, she made friends mainly with neighbors in the various apartment buildings where we lived. Some of these relationships led to close friendships which lasted for many years. There were always two or three couples with whom my parents vacationed, but never a whole circle of friends. If my father resented this narrowing of his circle, he did not show it. Instead, my parents developed an ever closer relationship to each other, a relationship that did not always leave room for a third partner, me.

They were, however as a unit, devoted parents, and they wanted the best for their only chick. This included sending me to a private, progressive school in Greenwich Village, recommended to them by one of my father's former artist girl friends. This school, still in existence today, stressed self expression, learning through experience, and democracy in the classroom. We learned our math by running the school store, improved our grammar and spelling by editing a small magazine, wrote and performed plays based on our reading of history, developed individual science projects, learned to bake bread by a recipeless trial and error method of cooking. We took numerous trips around Manhattan to learn how the city functioned and held endless classroom discussions to evaluate what we had seen. This mix worked well for me and developed in me a love of learning and of writing which has lasted a lifetime. Some students fared less well.

The founder and principal of the school was both a feminist and socialist, and these ideas permeated the classroom. Several of our teachers were probably members of the Communist Party in the 1920s. We saw a film of life in the Soviet Union, with emphasis on freedom for women, and a sequence of nude mixed bathing which surprised us (and indicates how early in the revolution it was made.) We also read the New Russian Primer. We were certainly not indoctrinated; the school was opposed to indoctrination of any kind, but we learned to view history through the lens of economic analysis. Who benefited and who lost out at the time of the development of city states? What role did the robber barons play in the development of the modern nation?

Above all, we learned that modern war was an abomination, that the munitions makers had alone benefited from World War I, recently ended, and that people everywhere had been the losers. Whole nations had been manipulated by war propaganda. We and other children everywhere must grow up with a determination never to allow war to happen again, and the courage to resist any efforts to change our minds.

These ideas were widely held in the 1920s and 1930s. Even among veterans of World War I, some of whom were friends of my parents, there was a strong feeling of disgust with militarism. My father was always somewhat apologetic about having joined the air force. Everything conspired to make me by age ten a committed pacifist.

This early pacifism had no link with religion. The philosophy of education behind the school I attended was very close to that of Professor John Dewey and pragmatism. Children were not only to learn from their own experience, they were to be spared the myths and superstitions of the past. We read the *Here and Now* books of Lucy Sprague Mitchell, who was an important patron of the school, and not fairy tales or Greek myths. Parents were encouraged to do the same at home; to avoid letting children go to the movies, (which were just beginning to come in) or even read the funny papers. I am sure the school never attempted to tell families how to conduct their children's religious education, but most of the children came from agnostic or humanist families, and religion simply never came up in the classroom, even in a historical setting.

My parents were more or less in sympathy with all these ideas. They were not very political, but they voted regularly for Norman Thomas and subscribed to mildly socialist, though certainly not Communist, ideas. Mother had never worked for suffrage, and had left her nursing to devote full time to being a housewife, but she was enough of a feminist to urge me to make a career for myself in the world, and not spend my time in what she described as the petty work of women. In terms of religion they taught me that God is love, that Jesus was a good man, that the best of religion was expressed in good human relationships, and that much of the rest was narrow and superstitious. They liked to listen to Harry Emerson Fosdick on the radio, but they rarely went to church, and while they allowed me to go to Sunday school when I was visiting my Canadian relatives they did nothing about it in New York.

And yet I had as a child, moments which I now regard as openings; feelings of intense identification with the whole of creation, of the expansion of self into the universe as I looked up into the heavens on a starry night. I had no concept of God onto which to hang these feelings; they seemed to have no relation to the stern old man with a beard whom my mother had rejected. Rather the spirit I felt at these moments was warm, nurturing, growthful, motherlike. The universe was on my side, I dimly felt. The ocean, in which I loved to dive and swim, would sustain me, bear me up, heal me of any hurt, carry me safe toward shore. My early writing, blank verse and word pictures, were of the glitter of ice on a frosty night, the swoop of a seagull. They were poems of praise, though whom or what I was praising I did not try to understand.

There was a dramatic change in my family, and in me, at the time of the Great Depression. During the 1920s my father had done quite well as a free lance artist, working for newspapers and magazines, and doing a lot of book jackets. But with the coming of the depression the sources of his commissions dried up. He made the usual rounds of art editors, and came home empty handed. His confidence sagged and with it his health, which had never been strong since he was wounded in the air crash in World War I, now collapsed.

I was still quite young when all this began to happen, and my memories are hazy, and fasten on physical things; the sight of the bread line around St. Vincent's Hospital, the men defeated, slouching. Winter sun glinting on the tin roofs of Hooverville on a frosty morning. Our furniture sitting out on the street as we moved from our nice apartment on 12th Street to a not very nice one on 9th and Perry.

Among my parents' close friends at this time was a new couple who were also feeling the pinch. Unlike earlier friends of theirs, Topsy and Frank were quite religious, and were currently interested in the Oxford Group Movement. This was an international religious revival movement in the Thirties among middle class and upper middle class people, which stressed seeking the will of God in Quiet Times, confessing sins to one another, and striving for the Four Absolutes: Absolute Purity, Absolute Honesty, Absolute Unselfishness and Absolute Love. While non-denominational it had close roots and ties with the Anglican Church in England and the Episcopal Church in the United States.

In their troubles, my parents began attending some of the meetings of this group, my father (who had a mystic streak) with more enthusiasm, I think now, than my mother. We had Quiet Times with Frank and Topsy, and sometimes within our own small family. We began to attend a local Episcopal church, where an early branch of AA was also coming into being, and my father decided to be baptized along with me.

By this time I was thirteen, old enough to go alone to the Sunday school at Trinity Church on Sunday mornings. I remember the walk through the deserted New York streets better than anything that happened at the church Sunday mornings, but the experience must have been positive, for later I returned to the Episcopal church and became quite religious for a time.

Things had not improved for my father, and we were reduced to real poverty, sometimes living on the tiny pension he received from the Royal Canadian Air Force. My mother decided at this point to seek work as a nurse, but even nurses were in surplus supply, and those jobs available went first to nurses trained in the USA. My father was diagnosed as having pernicious anemia, which was to be treated with liver injections. There seemed to be no solution but to move to his home in Tampa, Florida and live with my grandparents for a while until the injections began to work.

I had sympathized with my parents' dilemma up until this point, but now I was upset and angry about the thought of leaving the school and the friends I loved. My best friend's parents generously offered to keep me if I could stay another year and graduate, but my parents would not hear of it. I could not discuss it with my mother, but my father had always been my friend. I remember telling him how unhappy I was, and seeing him, to my horror, burst into tears. He had always been my hero, my support. Why had he let life push him around like this? Determination that I would never let this happen to me, that I would show the world for his sake, took root.

We moved to Florida, and I was miserable. My mother and grandmother did not get on well, and none of the three of us could stand the intense heat of summer. My grandmother's efforts to introduce me to some grandchildren of her old friends failed. I was a total misfit; a gangly thirteen-year-old kid with pigtails, a fondness for writing poetry and modeling horses out of clay, and an economic view of history; the girls with whom I went to school were older than I, already belonging to the secret societies that were part of social life all over the South, wearing silk stockings, perming their hair, and talking about boy friends and the next tea dance. Besides, ethnic lines were now tightly drawn, and the fact that my grandmother was Jewish, which was acceptable in her day, was not in mine.

For a while I was virtually ostracized. I could have joined a circle of Jewish girls, but I did not feel myself sufficiently Jewish to make that work. There were a few unattached girls, but they were prideful and prickly. My parents seemed as puzzled by my dilemma as I. My mother kept urging me not to care, and to feel myself above those who excluded and sometimes teased me, but it was hard advice for a teenager to take.

It was during this period that I found myself at odds with everyone over the issue of race. Perhaps the fact that I was an outsider myself made me sensitive to exclusion. There had been no Blacks at my school in Greenwich Village, and race never seemed to have come up, except as a topic of classroom discussion. I assumed that my parents felt as I did, but early in our stay in Tampa I learned differently. Having taken a walk by myself at night, I returned to find my mother frantic and my father joining my grandparents in telling me that I now lived in the South, where things happened to white girls and women who were not protected. My grandmother's neighbors paid their Negro help a dollar a week, and grumbled that they were lazy. I even heard occasional hints that lynchings still took place and were regrettable but brought about by the attitudes of "uppity Niggers." The fact that the Negroes had to sit at the back of the trolleys, the complete segregation of movies houses and other public places became painful to me.

I remember vividly one day when I was out in the yard behind the building in which we occupied a small apartment, drying my hair in the sun. A rather stout and red faced man I hadn't seen before came out of a neighboring building and got into his car. An elderly Black man was passing through the yard at the time, I believe to attend to a neighboring lawn. The Southerner started up his car, and all but knocked down the Black man. Perhaps it was by mistake, but seeing the Black man jump he roared with laughter, and began to do it again and again, chasing the Black man over the yard with his car. I remember leaping to my feet with my fists clenched and my heart beating violently wanting to intervene, but not knowing how, watching in sick despair until the Black man finally escaped through the hedge.

Perhaps there were others who felt as I did, but I had no way of contacting them. In frustration I turned to the local Episcopal Church, hoping to find at least some statement of moral values. At Young Peoples, made up primarily of social misfits like myself, I blossomed. I was the star of my communion class, and won the Bishop's cross for the best essay on local church history. I was able to talk about racism, though in the most general terms. I memorized the Nicene creed and much of the liturgy, I helped with Sunday school, I never missed early communion.

We had a wonderful priest at our local church, a saintly man, who believed in practicing the presence of God. Through his help, I was able to surmount problems of doubt, and give myself up to the worship. There were moments during communion, when I felt the sort of oneness with all creation which I had known as a child. And yet, though my heart was at peace, my mind was uneasy. I sometimes thought I was a hypocrite to repeat the creed when I knew in my heart of hearts I never had, and never could believe in some of its statements in regard to the resurrection. Young as I was, I could only accept much of the church's teaching as analogy or myth.

The church was an oasis for me, but the four years in Tampa remained difficult, and I longed to return to an environment like that of my Greenwich Village school. When I was a senior in high school I wrote to my former principal, asking where she thought I ought to go to college, and from her recommendations chose

Antioch in Yellow Springs, Ohio, a progressive college with a work-study program which would make it possible for me to earn much of my college tuition.

Arriving at Antioch in the fall of 1938 I felt I had come home again. People here seemed to regard me as a human being, not a representative of some club, race, or religion. My fellow students came from all over the United States, and were interested in ideas and in social concerns. Both the pacifism which I had first met in Greenwich Village, and the anti-racism I had developed on my own in Florida, seemed to be generally shared here and could find expression in campus activities. There was a campus civil liberties committee, and later an equal rights committee, which worked to improve relations with Blacks in the village of Yellow Springs, and to bring Black students to Antioch. A large portion of the student body seemed to be antiwar, and although we took a lively interest in the Spanish Civil War, and ate minimal "Bare Your Ribs for Spain" dinners in order to contribute to civilian relief, we were determined not be swept into a war hysteria, as our parents had once been. We felt sure we belonged to a generation that would never permit such madness to happen again.

To be sure, there were many differences in our pacifism, reflecting differences on the national scene. There was a religiously- based pacifism, which centered about the historic peace churches. The Quakers, Brethren, and Mennonites had always opposed war, and organized antiwar activities for their youth. The Quaker service organization, the American Friends Service Committee sent staff to visit college campuses and support students who opposed the war. Its director, Clarence Pickett, was a member of the Antioch board, and often spoke to the student body. The Quakers coupled this antiwar work with efforts to solve the problems overseas. They had sent a mission to Hitler to protest his treatment of the Jews, and were active in bringing Jews out of Germany and resettling them in this country.

In addition, there were pacifist groups in the Episcopal, Methodist, Presbyterian, Catholic and many other denominations. These groups tended to support the Fellowship of Reconciliation, organized by pacifists during World War I. The FOR at this period was interested in developing alternatives to violence, and was studying the methods which Mahatma Gandhi was using in India to struggle for Indian Independence.

Confusingly, the far Left was also opposed to war in the 1930s, regarding it as the tool of the imperialists. Like most college campuses of the time, Antioch had its Young Communist League, and its members were always at work trying to control the campus peace movement to make it serve Party ends. They were not very effective in this effort, and were sometimes rather ludicrous in their strategies. There were, however, a number of mildly radical students who did not draw a very sharp line between the Leftist and the philosophical pacifist position.

From the fall of 1938, to the spring of 1940, this uneasy alliance persisted, giving us a great sense of solidarity among students. Then Hitler attacked the USSR, and overnight, the pacifists on the Left became militarists. A delegation from Antioch left the campus to drive to Washington D. C. in June of 1940 to attend a nationwide student peace conference. When they arrived, they discovered its name had been changed to a people's conference, and the agenda was now how to support the USSR in its war effort against Hitler. I was in New York City at the time, on my way to a job waiting table in the Adirondacks. I attended the rally in Central Park, but the young man whom I heard speak was an isolationist, and therefore unaffected by the switch. Back on the Antioch campus the following fall our small Young Communist League brought in a speaker who said in effect that all pacifists should now be regarded as traitors, and should be hanged.

The isolationists, were also, for a time, strange bedfellows. The America First Committee, active in this period, believed that the United States ought not to get involved in the European struggle out of self interest. Some members of the America First Committee also expressed anti-Semitic, even fascist views, so it was looked on askance by most people of liberal persuasion. But it was a factor on some college campuses, and it managed to insert the question of the likelihood of invasion into the antiwar debate.

At Antioch, we were all much influenced by a sociology professor, Dr. M. N. Chatterjee, from India, who espoused a Gandhian view of war. Evil must be resisted, Gandhi believed; there was no room for self-serving, isolationist sentiments. But it must be resisted through means which would ultimately change the heart and nature of the oppressor. Conflict was inevitable; but society needed new means to resolve conflict which did not create fresh problems. War was a crude method; better methods must be created. The peace movement had languished because it had failed to come up with an alternative to violence. By aggressively seeking to solve problems through nonviolent means, by being willing to accept, but not inflict violence, one brought a new factor to the equation; the factor of truth.

The methods of nonviolence, Chatterjee taught, did not come naturally. One had to be trained. To train his nonviolent workers, Gandhi had established small centers, called ashrams, where men and women could be trained in nonviolence, deepen their spiritual lives, and support themselves by growing their own food. Families of nonviolent workers would be cared for at the ashram, in the event that the mother and/or father was jailed in the struggle. Chatterjee encouraged his most devoted disciples at Antioch to found such an ashram in the spring of 1940. The mother of one young man owned a farm in Northeastern Ohio, and here in June, Ahimsa took shape.

As in most similar communitarian experiments, at Ahimsa a great deal of time was taken up in the complexities of daily living; planting a garden, building an additional cottage, milking the goats, trying to raise chickens. There were endless discussions about how to live communally and still retain some personal privacy. People arrived who wanted to join the community, but brought personal problems with them. Most members of the core group were still in school, trying to balance work at Ahimsa with courses and with earning a living of some nature.

Yet in its eighteen months of existence, Ahimsa managed to conduct an experiment in nonviolence when some of its members participated in a successful attempt to integrate a swimming pool in Garfield Park, in nearby Cleveland. James Farmer, who would later play a major role in the nonviolent civil rights group, was a participant in this effort. Members of the group lobbied against the passage of the conscription bill in October of 1940, and later launched two nonviolent marches across Ohio, Pennsylvania, and New York, gathering food to be sent to civilian sufferers in Europe. Ahimsa attracted the lively interest of A. J. Muste, Muriel Lester, Ralph Borsodi, and many other of the leading pacifists of the day. Ideas were explored here, such as the use of nonviolence in civil defense in the case of invasion, which were not addressed in Peace Studies until quite recently. In the history of the development of interest in nonviolence in this country Ahimsa deserves a place of recognition.

I was studying political science, as a background for journalism, and I did not have any classes with Dr. Chatterjee. I was never more than peripheral to the Ahimsa experiment, but I became interested in the theory of nonviolence, and tried to incorporate it into the papers I wrote for my political science professor. Sometime in the late fall of 1941 I spent a weekend at Ahimsa, meeting the remaining members of the community, and hearing about its past.

Having lost their fight against conscription, which they believed would lead this country itself closer to the fascism it was supposedly fighting, members of the Ahimsa community one by one were faced with the draft. A few applied for conscientious objector status and were rejected. Others believed that it was wrong to cooperate with conscription by accepting conscientious objector status. The whole theory of nonviolence was based on the refusal of the individual to cooperate with the state. These men refused to register, or refused induction either into the army or alternative service, and consequently were jailed, brought to trial, and sent to prison for their noncompliance.

As the war in Europe became more deeply joined, and Jewish refugees arrived with their tales of Hitler's persecution, the size of the pacifist group at Antioch dwindled. More and more of our fellow students became persuaded that only force could stop Hitler.

It was a rather small and a very somber group that gathered at the home of a pacifist professor on the night of December 7, 1941, to reflect on what the attack on Pearl Harbor meant to us, and what our role would be, now that the United States was at last at war. Would fascism come to this country, as we had sometimes predicted? Would we be hunted down and persecuted for our antiwar sentiments? Would we yield? Should we go underground and keep in touch? I had never liked being in the minority, and a cold shiver went down my spine.

As a woman I did not of course have to face the draft, but most of the young men with whom I had gone to the movies or to college dances were conscientious objectors and I was concerned for their sakes. Recently my interest had narrowed and was concentrated on one of these. Allen first drew my attention when I discovered that superficially at least he came from a background somewhat similar to mine. His father was an architect, as mine was an artist, and he had also gone to a progressive school. He came from a Quaker family, but confessed he didn't know quite how he felt about religion. He was popular among his fellow students and much sought after by young women. It was rumored on campus that he had been invited to several debutante parties. To me he seemed a blend of the things I had valued in my New York past, and the social status I had longed for in vain while I lived in the South. I kept arranging for ways for our paths to cross. At about the time of Pearl Harbor I finally succeeded in attracting his interest and in developing a friendship with him which rapidly grew close in the hectic months of early 1942.

Allen was a member of the Ahimsa group, and had struggled with the question of whether to register for the draft. As a Quaker he would face no difficulty persuading his draft board to assign him to c.o. status. Yet he wondered if he ought to register at all, reasoning that the draft itself was a step toward totalitarianism, and to cooperate with it was not in keeping with the philosophy of nonviolence. He also believed that conscientious objector status ought to be granted to anyone who felt he could not fight, for either religious or philosophical grounds, and believed it was unfair for him to cash in on his Quaker heritage while a very good friend, equally dedicated to peace, was being sent to jail. In the end, he had decided to register as a c.o., but he continued to feel guilty about it.

Allen's Quaker ancestors had settled in New Jersey in colonial times and had consistently upheld the Quaker peace testimony, generation after generation. During the Civil War, one great grandfather had refused on conscientious grounds to manufacture blankets for the union troops. Allen's own parents had gone to Germany at the end of World War I to help feed the starving children of the former enemy. Allen's first language as a toddler was German. Two of his aunts had worked with refugees during the Spanish Civil War. While in college he had worked for the American Friends Service Committee in Student Peace Service, traveling from campus to campus to urge college students to think about peace issues. His two brothers were both opposed to war.

Recognition of the right of Quakers and others to conscientious objection to war had come slowly. During the Civil War religious conscientious objectors had the choice of paying a bounty of $300 so that other men could fight in their places, or being drafted into the army despite their principles. Most refused to pay the bounty. A few were assigned to nursing service, but others were drafted into the army and then disciplined, even tortured, when they refused to bear arms. During World War I there was still no clear-cut provision for conscientious objectors. An uncle of Allen's was threatened with death by an angry sergeant for refusing to carry a gun. Fortunately he was able to get in touch with the American Friends Service Committee, just organized to provide alternative service for religious objectors, and was furloughed from the army and sent overseas to France. Other c.o.'s were not so fortunate, and slipped through the safety net.

With the coming of World War II the peace churches worked closely with the Selective Service to develop a system under which those whose conscientious objection was based on religious grounds could obtain exemption from military duty upon being drafted, and be sent to do alternative national service in Civilian

Public Service Camps. The concept of CPS was that of William James, providing a moral equivalent to war. The men were assigned to "work of national importance" which was being neglected because so many other men were drafted. Work for the U.S. Forestry Service, in replanting trees and fighting forest fires, work for the Department of Health against hookworm by building latrines in hookworm infested areas, serving as guinea pigs in medical experiments, helping to operate state institutions which were short staffed, were among the forms alternative service took. In most cases the c.o.s could not see that their work had national importance, or any sort of importance whatsoever. The camps were located in isolated areas to avoid contact and friction with the local community, and the men were given an allowance of only $2.50 a month, and were not supposed to work to supplement this tiny sum, since it meant mingling with the community. There were many rules curtailing leaves and travel, which the camp director and his assistant, working for one of the peace churches, was obliged to enforce on frustrated, unhappy men.

Facing the draft, many young couples throughout the United States were plunging into marriage in 1942. On the Antioch campus alone there were something like thirty weddings that June. We decided, on rather short notice, to be married, and so informed our parents. Allen and I had a year to go before graduation, but I was twenty-one and he was twenty-two; old enough to make our own decisions as we told them. We did not allow ourselves enough time to be married under the care of the local Friends meeting, as Allen and his parents would have liked, but we married ourselves after the manner of Friends, asking a local minister to be silently present in order to sign the wedding certificate. We wrote our own service, adapting the one traditionally used by Friends. We were sufficiently unsure of our beliefs that we left out the phrase, "in the presence of God," and substituted "promising" instead "to be true to our common ideals." But we knew that someday we would return to the search for spiritual grounding in which we were both engaged. Meanwhile we had our immediate future to think of. We would support ourselves by alternately working and studying during our senior year, but we knew that after Allen's graduation in 1943 he would shortly be drafted, and sent to one of the CPS camps. Wives were not permitted to live in, or even very near, these camps. The idea was that the c.o.s ought to be willing to make the same sacrifice as men drafted and sent overseas away from their wives and children. Theoretically it made sense, but practically it seemed like a senseless rule, causing undue hardship to demoralized men, and leaving wives with small children without any means of financial support. Allen's older brother was married and the father of two small children, and when he was drafted it was necessary for his wife to live with her parents-in-law in order to survive.

CPS certainly did not sound very attractive to us, and we began to look for ways we could be together during the war years. One alternative was to serve in Mexico, working in rural villages for the American Friends Service Committee. We were actively exploring this option when a congressman added a rider to a bill which forbade all conscientious objectors from leaving the country. Another possibility we briefly explored was to work in the internment camps to which Japanese-Americans from the West Coast were being sent in a wave of wartime hysteria which overlooked fundamental American civil liberties. But it soon became apparent that the most important service the Quakers could render, in addition to protesting, was to arrange for the relocation of students from the camps to colleges out of the disputed zone, and in this work there was no room for idealistic but inexperienced college students. It began to appear that there was no way out; we would face separation along with many other young couples throughout the United States.

Besides worrying about our future, and finishing our courses we were involved that last year in an effort to bring Black students to Antioch. Founded in the nineteenth century by Christian idealists, and headed by the noted educator, Horace Mann, Antioch had originally opened its doors to Black students as well as pioneered in paying men and women faculty equally. The interracial tradition had died out, however, and it was many decades since a Black student had even applied to Antioch. We worked with a woman faculty member to raise scholarship funds to make Antioch attractive to Black students, and to try to develop what links we could with the Black community. The year after we left the first Black student, Edythe Scott, came to Antioch, to be followed several years later by her younger sister, Coretta, who married Martin Luther King, Jr.

We left Antioch College in March of 1943 and moved to New York City where we both had entry level jobs in the consumer cooperative movement. I had completed all my course work; Allen had to write some papers. By the end of June we were graduates, by the first of August Allen was drafted and assigned to a forestry camp in upper Michigan administered by the Brethren Service Committee. He made this choice because of his interest in consumer cooperatives since the Michigan camp had an imaginative education director who was running a school on cooperatives for the men after hours.

After Allen had been at Valhalla for three months the camp was broken up, and he transferred to Sykesville. I continued to work in New York City and it was possible for us to spend an occasional weekend together, sometimes in New York, sometimes in Baltimore, and sometimes at Sykesville. The occasions were hectic, and tinged with an element of strain. When we first moved to New York City we had begun to discover some differences in ourselves we had not faced before. Returning to Greenwich Village was for me regaining paradise lost; I could forgive the city its dirt and sounds and smells because I loved it so much. I had always intended to make it my home, and to send my children to my beloved school. Allen however had never lived in a big city, and didn't like it very much. Other differences began to emerge, to our bewilderment. We had only known each other on the Antioch campus where we seemed in accord on everything; perhaps we ought to have waited as our parents had warned, until we had had more time to get acquainted.

I had idealized Allen before we were married, and during that first year I had been trying hard to be like him, and like the members of his family I had met. I had never known Quakers before I went to Antioch, confusing them in my mind with the Amish. Instead I found those at college delightful, cosmopolitan, and well informed. Their practical approach to social problems appealed to me and their experiential approach to religion seemed the answer to the puzzle I had been trying to solve for myself for a long time. I began to attend the small campus meeting for worship, held in Rockford Chapel. I found in the silence an opportunity for the sort of religious experience I longed for without the necessity of giving that experience words. I thought I would like to forge a whole new identity as a Quaker; this urge had much to do with my interest in Allen originally.

But trying to be like Allen meant not expressing my whole self, I discovered. Allen and his relatives tended to shy away from the direct expression of feeling, and to raise their eyebrows a little at others who spoke with passion. There was a blandness about them I could not seem to emulate. When Allen left for CPS camp I missed him dreadfully, but I also felt a sort of relief, a permission to please no one but myself for a while. I was still very young, and wartime New York was fun; I sometimes found myself flirting with other men, just as though I were not committed to Allen, in a way that frightened me, and certainly upset him when I told him about it.

Besides, I was finding life as the wife of a conscientious objector in wartime Manhattan increasingly difficult. When I looked up old school friends I discovered that their husbands were overseas, and when I met my parents' old colleagues they turned out to be deep in civilian defense. Several told me in as kindly tones as possible that they felt Allen was making a great mistake. Yes, they had been against war, but this war was different. How did I propose to stop Hitler? My answers about nonviolent defense didn't sound very compelling even to me. I tried going to Quaker meeting once or twice, but I was very new to Quakerism, and the meeting I attended did not seem much like the one at Rockford Chapel.

I decided finally to join Allen to see if in the Sykesville setting we could not recapture the perfect union we had experienced at

Antioch; if I could not recommit myself to wartime pacifism, if I really believed what I had so confidently stated I believed when I wrote my senior paper. Sykesville was to be the laboratory where I tested myself and my faith. And that is ultimately what Agnes Holler helped me do.

Chapter III

*A*FTER I LEFT THE TB WARD, I was assigned to II-D, the women's infirmary ward on the second floor of the Hubner building. This ward was ruled by Mrs. Porter, a stern but good-tempered matron from the village nearby, who did church work in her off hours, owned her own home, and clearly felt herself to be a cut above the regular attendants. It was her ambition to have the cleanest, neatest, quietest ward in Hubner, and though she succeeded in maintaining sparkling floors and freshly washed windows, it was hard on the poor bewildered souls in her charge who were constantly herded out of the way of the floor waxers. She did not seem very pleased to have me come on the ward, and she treated me as some sort of overgrown, difficult child. She was always correcting me, gently but firmly, for scuffing my feet as I walked down the freshly waxed hall, or not screwing the lids back tightly enough on the jars of Klomine, the disinfectant with which we washed the floors before we waxed them. Since my own mother had been critical of me for similar offenses I felt myself to be always in the wrong, and clumsy to boot. I worked hard to please her, but I never quite achieved this goal, nor felt I had much dignity.

As the infirmary, II-D housed any woman patient in the Hubner building who became ill enough to need nursing care. One young schizophrenic woman from the violent admissions ward, South II-A, was brought to us when she was about to have a baby, and kept there for several weeks after the birth. She was a beautiful woman, but very disturbed. They took the baby away from her immediately after its birth, and she kept getting up, and walking, naked, to the bathroom to wash out her blood soaked sanitary pads in the common toilet. A woman whose leg had been broken in electroshock therapy treatment came to us, and had to be restrained in bed until the leg could be cast.

But most of our patients were what we then called senile, brought in by despairing husbands and heart-broken, guilt-ridden daughters who could no longer cope with them at home. People referred to senility as a form of second childhood but I quickly saw how dismally far from happy childhood these poor souls were. Anxiety seemed to be their prevailing mood; a horrid anxiety that drove them to endless repetitions of bizarre behavior, to persistent wanderings and questionings, and back sometimes in desperation to the comforts of childhood. One fat old woman masturbated endlessly, and a very small, dried-up old woman sucked her thumb. Much more usual however was a woman like Mrs. Hooper who came twenty times an hour to the nursing station to ask plaintively, "Where am I? When will they come to take me home?"

It wasn't hard on II-D to imagine oneself in the patient's place; to know what it might be like to wake up in a strange bed, in a strange place, with noisy strangers all about you, and not be able to understand what it was all about, nor get a coherent answer from any of the nurses—if indeed they were nurses—who pushed you around, sometimes quite roughly. And to feel at the same time that your faculties were slipping, that you couldn't hear, or see or understand. It was clearly a nightmare for these women, and the well-waxed floors and polished windows did nothing to relieve their panic. The attendants in fact did little for them but to hurry them through the routines of the day, keep them out of the way of the wax polisher, and administer a heavy dose of Paraldahyde at night.

Within a week of my being transferred to II-D one of our patients died. She was a very old woman, her eyes filmy with cataracts, and one leg gangrenous. A bevy of doctors came to see her one morning, and after that her family was called. A small middle-aged man who might have been her son sat by her bedside that afternoon, but she was in a coma, and unresponsive, so he left when visiting hours were over. After that I was assigned to stay with her. Her temperature was high, her pulse fluttered, her breathing was strange. I had never seen a person die, and I was both frightened and fascinated. I searched my heart in vain, however, for any shred of compassion; it seemed to me that this woman's life had ended long ago, and the long drawn out process of dying was simply hard on those who had to attend her. Namely, me. I was shocked at this reaction in myself, but there it was, I was unfeeling.

Towards the end of the afternoon Mrs. Porter relieved me while I ran an errand for her at the dispensary. When I returned, the woman had died. She seemed little different than she had before, except no breath disturbed her face, her temperature had fallen, and the odor of her leg was suddenly much worse. Briskly Mrs. Porter got to work showing me how to fix the corpse so that it could be taken down to the small morgue in the basement; the apertures had to be stuffed with cotton, hands and legs tied loosely, jaw tied so it would not be open when the body stiffened. I thought for a bit that I was going to be sick, but I managed to turn away to get occasional gasps of fresher air. After we had finished our work we rolled her onto a stretcher, covered her with a fresh sheet, and I took her down on the elevator to the basement morgue, where bodies were kept in a sort of slide-in-refrigerator until the undertaker came for them. I just had time to return to II-D, change the linen on the bed, and wash my hands before it was time to meet Allen for supper.

I approached him with a grin of triumph on my face. I wanted to tell him I had seen a person die, and taken care of a corpse, all with matter of fact dispatch. Later, however, I thought again and again about the incident and about the fact that I had been so unfeeling in the face of death. Was I only able to experience life through my mind? Was the writer's habit of translating all experience into words, words, words, standing between me and true feeling?

I tried writing about detachment, first a poem and then a story, but neither came off, precisely because there was so little feeling attached to the concept. But the writing in turn made me more conscious of the fact that I was indeed retreating from the life of the ward, attending instead more and more to a procession of words that ran through my head, describing my experience to myself in the third person. "Now she is walking down the corridor to get the mop. A patient approaches her but she knows what the question is and she doesn't have time to answer." Was this possibly some schizophrenic trait I was developing? I touched my keys more frequently.

On the other hand, detachment was a big help in getting through the long, boring days, in not getting too mad at Mrs. Porter when she turned off the patients in order to clean house, or when she spoke to me as though I were a child. Detachment also removed me from sights and smells that would otherwise make me sick, and there were plenty of those on II-D.

The morgue in the basement of Hubner served the whole hospital, patients being brought from the men's group and women's group to await removal by the family, or in many cases, burial in the public burial ground. As often as possible the doctors obtained permission to perform autopsies, and occasionally medical students came from Baltimore to participate. After the doctors were finished it was the job of the attendants to sew up the bodies and prepare them for the undertakers. Whether out of malice, or because she wondered if I were good for anything else, Mrs. Porter often volunteered me for this assignment.

To touch the icy, green-white flesh of a corpse was bad enough, but to take a needle and thread, and sew up the gaping abdomen, as one would a Christmas turkey, was the most difficult task I had ever performed. Usually another attendant was assigned to the job with me, and by talking quickly, and not watching my hands, I was able to get through with it. Once or twice though I was alone, and the chill of the room combined with my just-below-the-surface panic to make my teeth chatter as I worked. At times I could scarcely believe it was really me that was doing this thing. I remembered a girl who had played field hockey, had sat for hours in the college library, and worn gardenias to proms, and it did not seem possible that these two selves were really connected. And yet I did the things I was asked to do, and took pride in proving that the wife of a c.o. need not be a coward, and put it all behind me in order to present Allen with a smiling face.

It was out of the dynamics of this strange time that I wrote my first really strong short story. For some reason I had two hours together off one afternoon, and I spent them at a typewriter in the social service office, where I was welcome because of my future status as a social worker. I sat down without any thought at all in my head and batted out a story about a little girl of divorced parents who maintained a dream world about her father, and guarded it jealously from the impact of reality when her father came home and showed no interest in her. I saw absolutely no connection between the story and my own life. My parents had never been divorced, and were in fact devoted to each other, sometimes to the exclusion of their only child. Only years later did I surmise that the story represented my little girl's longing to have my father to myself, and its accomplishment only in a dream world. At the time, I only knew it was good. I called it *The Secret Story* and sent it off to the *Ladies Home Journal*. Six weeks later I got it back with a long letter, saying the editorial board had been divided about publishing it, but the decision was that it was too "terrible" for their pampered readers. Wouldn't I, however, write another story, soon and send it in?

I was elated beyond measure by this encouragement and spent much of my time off writing, but nothing measured up to that first story, and it was a good many years before I was published in the *Ladies Home Journal*. Nevertheless, day dreams about becoming an author instead of a journalist began to possess me, and help me endure Mrs. Porter and the Klomine and the endless complaints of the patients.

The only place to sit down in II-D was in the nurse's office and here Mrs. Porter ruled regally, making up charts, and gossiping with her visiting friends. It was more than I dared to go in and take a seat in the corner. I managed therefore to stay on my feet all day, grabbing a polisher to help perfect the glistening floors when there was no other way to keep occupied. It was no use talking with the patients; they were too disturbed to converse, and I had neither the authority or the knowledge to do anything to relieve their anxieties.

The Maryland spring flowered and deepened while I worked on II-D, and summer came. Suddenly it was hot, very hot. In our little room in the attendants' quarters it was impossible to sleep unless we opened the door to the hall to gain a little ventilation. Other attendants had the same problem; soon we devised the plan of making a half door of wood covered with burlap, and opening the heavy outer door before we settled for the night. The other c.o. couples following suit, and the hall soon blossomed with variations of the half door. The regular attendants who shared the quarters with us of course disapproved and kept their doors tightly shut.

Privacy was hard to come by on the attendants' ward. We shared one large old-fashioned bathroom, across the hall from us, and learned to listen intently for the sound of an opening door so that we could pop in and take our turn. One of the c.o. wives liked to do her washing in the bathroom, and took what seemed like hours, as others impatiently waited. Worse, our immediate neighbors were an old time Sykesville couple who disapproved of the conchies, and expressed their feelings in slammed doors and tight lips. Sometimes at night, if we were making love, the bedsprings would squeak, and these neighbors would pound on the wall for silence. It was embarrassing, and might have been inhibiting, if we had not been so young.

With the coming of the hot weather, the regular staff began to take their annual vacation, and help on the wards, already in short supply, was further depleted. I was detached from Mrs. Porter, to the dismay of neither of us, and used for relief, going from ward to ward to cover as the remaining attendants took their day or their hours off.

There were four women's wards in the Hubner group; South II-A, the violent disturbed ward; South II-B, for slightly less disturbed patients; East Ward on II-D, the infirmary ward; and II-C, the convalescent open ward. I was on II-C twice and found it depressing. The patients were close enough to being normal to have lost the color and excitement of their madness. Instead they were as a group self enclosed, uncommunicative, and resentful of the attendants. I found them uninteresting; only years later did I begin to understand the desperate struggle for pride and self confidence that must have been going on beneath the surface of those blank exteriors.

South II-B was supposed to be a relatively calm ward, but I never found it so. There were altogether too many highly-disturbed women in the admissions wing to crowd them all onto the disturbed ward; at best, South II-B got those who were not deemed likely to commit physical violence. We had, nevertheless, our share of patients who shouted obscenities from the windows, or paced, or made random rushes at the door, and there was often a patient hit by sudden panic who had to be led, or dragged into the neighboring bedlam.

Electroshock therapy was in its heyday, and Sykesville, which prided itself on having the newest and best of everything among state mental hospitals, used it extensively, and indiscriminately. Both Allen and I were assigned to assist giving shock treatment— he far more frequently—and both of us came to hate the sight of the shock box, and to fear its results for our patients.

The routine was always the same. Every morning the patients scheduled for shock therapy were told they could have no breakfast and then were gathered from their wards, and one by one strapped to a large leather trolley. Two attendants stood on either side of the patient to help with the strapping and to hold legs and arms during the treatment. The patient's head was then wired to the shock box by a device resembling a telephone headpiece, his or her temples having first been smeared with Vaseline. A linen towel was rolled and placed in the patient's mouth to serve as a gag, and when all was at last in readiness, the doctor threw the switch.

The victim then went into a convulsion so violent that she might have broken her own back or neck if we did not struggle to hold her steady. When the convulsion was at last over, the patient was unstrapped, flung limply onto a nearby cot, and allowed to sleep off the affects. He or she generally came to an hour or so later, and remained groggy and confused for the rest of the day.

One psychiatric theory at the time was that shock therapy interfered with sick patterns of thinking. After shock, the patients temporarily forgot everything, including their delusions, their *idees fixe*, even their depression. This confusion was supposed to give the ill man or woman a breather in which to learn new and better patterns of relating to himself and his fellow human beings. Given in conjunction with massive psychotherapy—this theory postulated—shock treatment could help patients establish healthier patterns. But even given without psychotherapy (which was in fact non existent at Sykesville) the shaking up of the synapses was somehow beneficial, a conjecture "proved" by the fact that many seemed to get better and were in fact able to go home. No studies were made on how many of the patients treated by shock therapy returned how soon to the hospital.

Whatever the theory, the patients regarded shock treatment as a form of cruel and unusual punishment. They hated and feared the little room in which the treatments were given, and relapsed quickly from their state of post shock confusion into their old patterns. We sympathized with them and came to oppose the treatment strongly, and to hate our involuntary complicity in it.

Some of the B ward women were still on a heavy dose of electro shock. Others got insulin shock treatment, and we had to give them a quick shot of sugar before they went into comas. Still others went to hydrotherapy in the basement where they were placed in wet packs, or given continuous tub baths. Sykesville was vigorous about providing some form of treatment for the patients during the early days of their admission, but it was hard to see from the attendant's point of view that any of the treatment was doing much good, or even managing to counteract the long days of turmoil on the ward.

Because the patients adapted at different rates, and because their symptoms took different forms, there were many extremes on South

II-B, from the erratic shouters to the quiet, contained women, pained by the noise and confusion. One nice looking young woman approached me on my first day on the ward and asked me quietly if it would be possible for me to arrange for her to speak with the doctor. It was all a horrible mistake, her being here at all. She was trying to make a good adjustment, but the noise and confusion was bothering her terribly, and it was impossible to sleep at night. Actually nothing was wrong with her at all; she had simply gone to her family doctor to see about some strange pains she was having in her stomach, and the doctor had sent her to a specialist, and ridiculous as this must sound, she had somehow gotten into the wrong office.

I was overwhelmed with sympathy for the young woman, but I knew my place in the pecking order of the hospital by this time, and it was not up to me to speak to the doctor. Had she asked the charge attendant, Mrs. Thomas, I asked? The young woman made a helpless gesture. "I did speak to her," she assured me. "But she has already had her mind poisoned against me. They shot her with rays, and she is in the plot."

I felt a prickling at the back of my neck. My own naiveté had led me into this. I still felt sympathy for the woman, but I obviously could not help her. I excused myself and walked off to other patients and other duties.

Every patient on every ward seemed to want to see the doctor. It was a natural request, but impossible to fulfill. When the doctor finally came on the ward to make his rounds he would stride through a chorus of begging women, spend a few minutes in the office looking at charts, issue orders for shock therapy, and stride out again. Like any state mental hospital, Sykesville was woefully understaffed; it was all the doctors could do to fill out forms, supervise the shock therapy, conduct admissions interviews, and deal with patients who were actually, physically ill. Otherwise they depended on rules, and the attendants to enforce them.

B Ward was separated by a heavy door from South II-A. From time to time the door shook with poundings, and we saw it open to admit flushed and bedraggled nurses and hysterical patients to the mutual hall. Occasionally a hyperactive patient was given a shot, but for the most part they suffered their frenzies unabated, and wild screams of anger, fear, and frustration rang down the halls. Nothing in my weeks at Sykesville had quite prepared me for the fear that assailed me the first day I was assigned to that ward.

C.o. wives had been tried out from time to time on South II-A but few had lasted. Instead, the ward was under the control of Mrs. Jones, a large, beefy charge nurse with the biceps and vocabulary of a drill sergeant, no chin, and pop eyes. She made no secret of the fact that she was not pleased to have the college kid assigned to her, nor was I able to hide my apprehension and dislike from her. I had only pride and determination to save me. I would not let them prove that c.o.s were yellow. I would do whatever I was asked, and somehow get through the days. I had tamed Agnes Holler, hadn't I?

It wasn't easy. Mrs. Jones believed implicitly that the patients only understood force, and the ward was in constant turmoil whenever she was in charge. The lock rooms, which downstairs in the men's violent ward where Allen worked now often sat open, here housed two or three patients at night, and often the patients were tied to their beds to restrain them. The day room was not much better. A few patients sat quietly on the hard chairs, sunk in their private worlds of terror, but the majority were noisy and hyperactive, assaulting each other, throwing chairs and trays of food at mealtime, screaming out of the windows at passersby, besieging the nursing station, hanging about the entrance door of the ward and making an effort to rush out whenever it was opened. Each month, several patients made it through that door, and once, one managed to elude her pursuers all the way down the hall, and leap from a second-floor balcony onto the cements steps below. She broke her pelvis, but not, as she had hoped, her neck.

Somehow in the midst of this chaos we went on with the hospital routines; reveille, medications, breakfast, baths, treatment, ward housecleaning, lunch rest, walk outdoors (for the very, very few who were allowed) medications, supper, bedtime. Even here, cleanliness was regarded as next to sanity, and we were forever plotting ways to give one bedraggled patient a shampoo, or clean another's fingernails. We even occasionally washed and waxed the floor, though it was necessary to lock the patients into side rooms left and right to do so.

I tried hard to do what I was told on South II-A, but Mrs. Jones' unremitting hostility toward me made me feel unsure of myself, and stupid. It sometimes seemed as though I couldn't win. Once I was asked to restrain an overactive patient by tying her wrists to her cot. I was given a pair of old silk stockings for this task, but no instructions. I tied the wrists as carefully as I could, but the patient fought me, and I managed to get the bonds too tight. An hour or so later I was called away from other duties by Mrs. Jones and marched into the lock room where the doctor sat, looking sternly down his nose at the woman's hands, swollen from the pressure of her bonds. Mrs. Jones folded her arms triumphantly while I was given a lecture by the doctor on the uses and misuses of restraint. Since Mrs. Jones herself used restraint indiscriminately and demanded that we do so also, the lecture seemed unfair, but I could not answer back.

A few days later I was in the doghouse again. A large blonde patient with a Swedish accent, evidently frightened to death by her surroundings, seized a floor polisher and began to swing it menacingly around her. The attendants stood about in a big circle, unable to approach her. Mrs. Jones called me and ordered me to take the polisher away from her. I managed to slip in somehow from behind and get a grip on her arm, once more relying solely on the holds I had learned in senior lifesaving drill. But the grip was imperfect, the woman was very strong, and I felt myself losing hold. I looked imploringly at the other attendants for help, but no one moved, and I finally lost my grip.

Just as I did, the doctor came upon the ward. "What's going on here?" he demanded, "Why isn't this patient restrained?"

Galvanized by his words, several of the attendants moved in simultaneously and the woman was removed to a lock ward. Then, in the doctor's presence, Mrs. Jones gave me a lecture on never releasing a disturbed patient. Hot words of self-defense rose to my lips, but I held them back. They would only have sounded apologetic, and would, I knew, make matters worse.

Much of the time I was on South II-A I was afraid, and knew I was afraid, and knew that the patients knew that I was afraid. It made me guilty and ashamed of myself. I still believed in non-violence but I was certainly not able to demonstrate the power of love over evil when I myself was full of fear. In fact, it became clear to me that love and fear were antithetical. I made myself a new aphorism; perfect fear casts out love. I could sense my fear was frightening the patients. "How terrible is this power that possesses me if it is so frightening to this attendant," I imagined they felt. And yet, there it was, a nasty fact about myself that could not be denied.

The first day I went to work on South II-A, one large dark-haired woman picked me out as the subject of her persecution. "There she is, she's a Russian spy," she screamed whenever I tried inconspicuously to whisk in and out of the day room. Another patient asked me if I was really a nurse, or just dressed up to look like one. I felt as though they were on to me, that my secrets were exposed by the insight which insanity gave them.

On the other wards, the women generally managed to cling to some shreds of their dignity. Here they let go completely, abandoning themselves to the dark currents of their madness. One theory advanced by the head of the Sykesville Social Service Department was that this was a very good thing; by allowing them an environment in which they no longer had any responsibility, in which they were free to let themselves go, the hospital made it possible for them to surrender the battle, to let the volcano blow, so that later it would be possible to restore the self on a new and stronger basis. It was the same philosophy that lay behind the justification for shock treatment. It sounded logical, until you allowed yourself to sense the terror and despair rampant on the ward. Then it began to sound like the old medieval theory of cure by torture.

And yet even here, even on South II-A, one came to know the patients as individuals. I remember one young woman with long blonde hair brought, struggling desperately with her captors, and so disturbed that she tore off all her clothes and had to be kept naked in a locked room. She was placed on a heavy schedule of shock treatment and kept locked up and heavily sedated. Coming and going from the ward as I was, I scarcely saw her for days on end. Yet somehow she learned my name, and one evening when I came on night duty she called me softly from the day room to look at the sunset. It was indeed memorable, a flush of peach across the distant hills, and above, the sky apple green with wisps of purple clouds. I came and stood beside her and we watched the colors deepen. Then someone began shouting in the bathroom and I had to leave her.

Emily, for that was her name, was fighting for control. I watched the brave battle at intervals during my harried days on South II-A, saw the tension in her every move, watched her flinch at every manifestation of violence against her. Yet she made it, step by step, up the ladder toward sanity; from the lock ward to the dormitory, from the day room to the privilege of a daily walk, finally, shakily from A ward to B ward.

Visitors came every Wednesday and Sunday, and patients were allowed to have visitors a month after their admission. Emily's month was up the weekend she moved to B ward. I was on night duty, but I had returned to the building in the afternoon to run an errand, and I passed her on the stairs. A pleasant looking woman, whom I took to be her mother, was there and with her two tiny blond children; a little girl, perhaps three with long blonde hair like Emily's and a sturdy little boy of two. Children were not allowed in the hospital, but the administration had evidently permitted Emily's mother to bring the children to meet her at the side door leading to the stairs. Emily was kneeling, an arm around each child, and when I saw her face, suffused with love and gentleness and regret, I had to turn away to hide my tears.

That night, after supper, I was sitting in the attendant's room, just getting my charts organized for the night, when two nurses came in from II-B, dragging a screaming, disheveled patient. It was Emily. Two attendants took her from the B ward attendants and thrust her into a lock room with another patient, then called for sedation. I stood at the window for a moment, watching the last glow of the sunset fade from the sky, and biting my lips.

The long nights of South II-A were an ordeal like none other at Sykesville. We were supposed to have at least three attendants on that ward at all times, but during the summer vacation period we occasionally didn't have a proper swing shift at night, so that when one attendant went on her hours we were down to two, and sometimes even to one. To be alone on South II-A in the dead of night was unlike being alone on the TB ward; there the perils were imaginary, here they were real. After a day of electroshock, of being yelled at by the powerful Mrs. Jones, the patients were stirred up, and often fought through their heavy doses of tranquilizers to disturbed wakefulness. One dared not leave the nursing station unattended, for there were always some recovering alcoholics on the ward who would drink the alcohol in which the thermometers sat, or attempt to get into the drug cupboard. And yet it did not take a sick imagination to conjure up disaster in the darkness beyond. Patients had been known to hang themselves in the bathroom or the lock ward, or cut or burn themselves elsewhere. Sometimes they hurt each other.

Occasionally in the course of the night, a disturbed patient would become so unruly we would be forced to call the doctor on night duty and ask permission to give her an additional sedative. Often the doctor was cross and drowsy and answered with a sleepy, "try more Paraldehyde." Sometimes he would come stumping on the ward, in his bathrobe if he lived in the building, which several did, and administer a hypodermic. It was hard to judge when to make such an appeal; I generally tried to manage without.

There were other horrors at night. South II-A was never house-cleaned as vigorously as the other wards. It was not possible in the turmoil of the days and the patients threw up, or were incontinent regularly. As a result we had armies of cockroaches which swarmed about the drains, and came out at night to make their nasty pilgrimages across the office wall. Once we moved the medicine chest, and there behind it the whole wall was alive and crawling. If and there behind it the whole wall was alive and crawling. If one were sitting at the desk, tired and half afraid, it was easy to imagine that the insects were ready to crawl across one's feet or land—as they occasionally did—on the pages of one's book.

Not that much reading got done. There was always some patient at the door. "Please call the doctor, I can't sleep." "Why do you have me locked up like this?" "Why aren't you getting ready for my wedding tomorrow?" The woman who took me to be a Russian spy spent one whole night guarding the entrance to the nursing station. My heart pounded as I slipped out past her to attend to other patients.

We did have an hour off at midnight for supper. But the supper, eaten in the attendant's dining room by the light of a few single bulbs suspended from the ceiling was a soggy and tasteless affair. It wasn't food that one needed anyway. Even the coffee seemed only to make one more sleepy and leaden at that time of night. The other night attendants were by and large a discouraging crew. The regular, career attendants chose daytime assignments, and the drifters, and alcoholics were left to watch the lonely hours of the night.

In charge of South II-A at night that summer was a c.o.'s wife, a pretty young woman from Lancaster county, who had married a young Brethren. I thought I would enjoy working with Lenore but I quickly discovered she had little use for other unit wives. Aside from her tie to her husband she felt herself more in sympathy with the regular attendants than with the members of the unit. From some of the regulars she had learned to treat the patients with amused disrespect, shoving them about as though they were so many unruly children, and snapping her fingers under their noses when they seemed inopportune or disobedient. It did not take me long to discover that underneath she was really very much afraid of them.

Lenore knew all the gossip of the hospital, and liked to repeat it. Did I know that Doris, the pretty blonde nurse, was going with one of the boys in the unit? Did I realize that her husband was overseas? Who did she think she was, anyway? Tongues were wagging all over the hospital. Why didn't the unit try to do something about it? I never knew what to say—indeed, what was there to say? I would try to change the subject, or desperately make some excuse to venture forth from the circle of light in the office into the threatening darkness in order to get away from her.

Watching Lenore taught me to accept my own fear. At least I recognized it, at least I did not turn it into a form of cruelty against the patients. But chiefly, the long nights on South II-A taught me I still had much to learn.

Chapter IV

I DREAMED CONSTANTLY WHILE I WAS AT SYKESVILLE. I had night-
mares about being lost on the wards, or losing my keys or
being attacked by patients. I had anxious dreams and guilty dreams
and angry dreams, and occasionally even happy dreams. It was as
though my inner self took courage, knowing that by day I was
surrounded by men and women whose inner selves were in charge
of their behavior, and chose this as a good time to communicate
with the outer, other me. Long years after I left the state hospital,
it continued to be the site of many of my dreams.

Our fellow attendants talked about the various stages of adjustment one went through. First there was the stage I had experienced on the TB ward, especially in relationship to Agnes Holler,
the stage of finding out that the work was bearable, that one could
do it. Then a stage where one began to discover that the patients
were not, after all, so different from the people on the outside.
Then the realization that one was, oneself, subject to many of the
same anxieties, fears, and torments which our patients dared to
express openly, to shout about, to act out. And finally the need to
find out what made one different from the patients. Coming down
to the discovery, "I am the one with the keys. It is that simple. I
keep the keys."

When I first went to work on the TB. ward, the patients seemed
one vast amorphous group. But as day followed monotonous day
they began to sort themselves out in my mind. One by one, I

learned their names and a little bit about their condition and their histories. Many had spent decades at the hospital, roaming the locked wards of the Women's Group, and were the gray, shapeless bundles that years of institutionalization produced. Their families had long since ceased to visit them, they were known to attendants only by a last name or a nickname; whatever had once distinguished them as human beings had apparently ceased to exist.

But there were a few younger patients who were more newly come to the hospital, as well as one or two older ones who had been transferred from a tuberculosis sanitarium. We had a patient labeled catatonic schizophrenic who sat in a rigid position, with one hand held high in benediction, and the second in her lap, grasping a bit of silk so tightly that we had to pry open the fingers by force to get at the sores underneath. There was a nice looking little old woman in an advanced state of paranoia who believed rays were being directed into her head to give her bad thoughts. There was a thin, hyperactive woman of middle years with a rasping voice who was described as a manic.

I was hungry, in those early days, for diagnoses and classifications. Fresh from college I believed that the way to master a new situation was to study it and learn its vocabulary. That was the approach that had worked most successfully for me for twenty-two years, and I saw no reason to think it might not work here. I read books about mental illness. I scanned the patients' charts eagerly for clues. Whenever possible I led fellow members of our unit into a discussion on psychiatric matters. One older unit member told me rather angrily that I ought to rely less on my head and more on my feelings, but it was not a remark I could understand at the time.

While there were some doctors who believed at this time that mental illness had a chemical basis, there were others who rejected this view, and thought that treatment of the psychotic could parallel that of the neurotic. We were passionately on the side of the latter view, and regarded shock therapy as a terrible form of rough punishment for confused men and women. A few of the doctors and social workers felt the hospital itself could function as a sort of therapeutic community, helping the patients to insight and recovery.

At the same time I was trying to understand the patients, I was getting to know the members of the Unit. The CPS unit at Sykesville was administered by the Church of the Brethren. The majority of unit members were either Amish or Brethren, belonging to one or another of the numerous sects into which those two churches were divided. Many came from Lancaster County, Pennsylvania and had the singsong cadence of the Pennsylvania Dutch in their voices. Like the patients, this group too seemed undifferentiated to me when I first arrived. I lumped them as kind and gentle people, but quite unlike myself and my friends. In time, however, I got to know them as individuals, and to understand the great variety of differences between the various sects to which they belonged.

There were some who were not allowed to travel by car at all, but used the buggies one sees on Lancaster County Roads. Others could own a car as long as it was black, and they painted the chrome black; some would wear buttons and some managed with hooks and eyes. One young couple belonged to a sect which had permitted them a few years of liberty as teenagers before joining the church and renouncing the world. Most opposed the war because scripture and their church had taught them war was wrong. They did not always understand our brand of pacifism. We envied them their surety, but knew there was no way we could ever return ourselves to their simple faith. We came to appreciate them, but felt that between us and them there was a barrier of reserve we could not always penetrate. We were young, and ourselves saw things in more simplified shades of black and white than we came to in later life.

This left us with a much smaller group of our fellow unit members from diverse backgrounds whom we seemed able to get to know more intimately. There was a young Methodist divinity student and his wife, an English professor from a small southern university, a liberal and questioning member of the church of the Brethren, a high-spirited young couple from Bethany College in

West Virginia, a folk dancing engineer from California, a Jewish dentist from Brooklyn, a middle-aged Salvation Army worker in social work training; a Philadelphia socialite, a Methodist radio mechanic and his wife from Florida, a Lutheran couple from Wisconsin, and our unit leader, Ralph.

Even among this more congenial group Allen and I felt ourselves somewhat outsiders. Most were more religious in a conventional sense than we were. We spent a great many more Sunday evenings singing hymns and having fellowship hours than we might have believed possible back in Greenwich Village days. As time went on, however, we found a still smaller inner circle of irreverent souls like ourselves who might join in the hymn singing but were ready to play poker night after night, to share an occasional bottle of wine, and to use the vocabulary we heard on the wards in new and funny ways. Something about the sobriety and dedication of our days seemed to demand this sort of release at night. In contrast to our more pious colleagues we felt like devils, and though the deviltry was pretty mild, it formed a solid bond of friendship.

While I was working on the infirmary ward in the Hubner building I was frequently asked to run errands. Allen and most of the other attendants were locked into the wards with their patients, but if I got through quickly at the dispensary or the hospital post office I could always drop in for a few minutes at the office of the unit director. Ralph was almost always in his shirt sleeves, pounding on the typewriter with gunfire hunt and peck blows. Selective Service, the Brethren Service Committee and the National Board for Religious Objectors all demanded endless forms and reports. Yet he was never too busy to stop, swing around in his swivel chair, and chat with whomever came to the doorway of his tiny office.

It was not hard to understand why Ralph had been chosen unit leader. He had a genuine warm interest in every member of the group, and a catholic taste in people which made him as much at home with the very conservative Mennonites as with our very few sophisticates. He himself came from a simple farm background, and belonged to one of the more liberal of the Brethren groups. Somehow, he had acquired a hunger and thirst for the world of ideas which had carried him quickly beyond the community of his upbringing. He liked to talk about the books he was reading, and since Allen and I and Sam were the greatest readers in the unit, he liked to drop into our room at night and talk or listen to music.

The thing that drew us all to Ralph, I think, was his never-ending high spirits. He was genuinely enthusiastic about the unit, and about the witness he believed we were making by our work to the hospital, and to the world at large of a moral alternative to war. He listened good naturedly to all the gripes and gossip, but he seemed to have the rare faculty of actually seeing the best in people. He never talked much about religion, but he had read Gandhi and Thoreau and believed that we were demonstrating the efficacy of nonviolence on the wards, and that was more important than our petty complaints.

A visit to Ralph's office was always a shot in the arm. I would tell him about Mrs. Porter's latest outrage, such as the day she kept all the patients in the dormitory all day so she could redo the floor of the dayroom, and he would laugh and agree that she was a better housekeeper than a nurse, and then perhaps give me something to read from another CPS unit in a state mental hospital. Or he would ask if I had ever read James Joyce, and if so, would I talk to him sometime about the *Dubliners*. Occasionally someone else would be at the doorway, getting cheered up, and I would note with just a pang, that Ralph seemed as interested in that person as in me.

Occasionally my errands took me down the front hall of the Hubner Building, past the administrative offices, and here, too, were friends. Helen, the red-haired wife of an older c.o., worked in the bursar's office and Sally, Adam's wife, was a secretary in the administrative pool outside the superintendent's office. Sally was a shy slender woman with flashing blue eyes behind glasses, and long brown hair. She worked conscientiously at her typing but she sometimes ran errands too, and stopped to talk with Ralph. I was always grateful to her for looking up from her desk when I passed, and giving me a warm smile.

Partly by chance, partly by design, members of our small circle worked together in the Hubner Building. Allen, Sam and Sandy were on the violent admissions ward, South 1A. Adam was charge attendant in South I-B. He was a little older than the rest of us, a little more ponderous. But we liked his wife Sally immensely, and we felt he was one of us. Besides Ralph, Ben, the dentist, had his chair in the basement also. Jim was on the swing shift.

Originally, it had taken five strong men to run the violent admissions ward, but after the c.o.s were placed there, the administration reduced the number to four, then to three. At the same time, the doctors were always hauling off one or another of the men to help with electric shock treatment, or to deal with a particularly violent woman patient in the ward above, so it was frequently the case that only two of the c.o. attendants were in charge of a ward of some forty patients, classified as highly disturbed.

The astonishing fact was that under c.o. administration, the level of violently disturbed behavior dropped markedly. Before the change, all four of the special locked isolation cells had been kept full, some with two or three patients jammed together to augment each other's madness. Now it was a rare day when more than one of these rooms was used at a time. The noise level, too, abated. While one could always hear the violent women's ward, above, far across the fields from the hospital, South I-A was relatively quiet.

What had happened to make the difference? When I first arrived, it seemed like some sort of miracle, but in time, after I had myself worked on the violent women's ward, and watched my reactions and those of some of the other attendants, I began to know some of the answers. For one thing, Allen and his friends were not afraid of their patients. Upstairs, among the women, one could trace a frightened attendant by the noise and uproar she created around her. I had discovered that I myself was sometimes a coward, my experience with Agnes not withstanding, and I learned from personal experience on South II-A how dangerous fear can be.

For another, the c.o.s genuinely liked their patients. At least Allen liked them, and I was secretly sure that it was his influence, his calmness and leadership, that quieted the ward. At night, in our little room in the Epileptic Colony, he would often speak of them, describing this one's improvement, that one's depression, another's visit from his wife. Allen's detachment and objectivity, his ability to leave himself and his interests out of relationships, which in some contexts I found bewildering, was a great source of strength on South I-A.

Occasionally, the stories he would bring home at night were amusing. One patient, encountered in the Men's Group on the hill, was always taking tender care of himself. He was pregnant and about to give birth to some baby rabbits. Another patient, Mr. Zepp, a lively manic, was often entertaining. One day Mr. Zepp began to draw madly with chalk upon the wall. The pictures were sketchy; one seemed to suggest a streak of lightning across a field.

"What's this, Mr. Zepp?" Allen asked.

Mr. Zepp pointed to a flat horizontal line. It was a field of wheat beaten down by hail, he explained. "That's a cheerless prospect."

"And what's this above the field?" Allen persisted.

"That's a ray of hope across a cheerless prospect." Mr. Zepp told him, running his words together. For the rest of our days at Sykesville, "A-ray-of-hope-across-a-cheerless-prospect" became a slogan.

After a series of shock treatments, Mr. Zepp improved and went home, a quiet, sober, sad little man under the wing of a large managerial wife, and we saw no more of him for a year. Then he returned, as excited and manic as ever.

But of course the stories were mostly tragic. There was Ted Johannsen, a tall handsome man, a graduate of Dartmouth, a veteran of the Navy, quiet, sensitive and intelligent, but convinced beyond all reasonable doubt that the walls were about to collapse upon him. Hour after hour, day after day, Ted stood braced in his isolation room, holding up the walls. Allen discovered that Ted had known some friends of his from Westtown School. He liked Ted, and spent hours talking to him. But companionship was not enough to reach the demons deep inside of Ted. He was given shock treatments, and after some weeks moved to a quieter ward. He seemed to be getting a little better. Then, one morning, they found him hanging in the broom closet.

The interest which the c.o.s took in their patients, and their willingness to listen was undoubtedly a factor in calming the violent ward. It also helped that the c.o.s in question were not working out personal problems on the ward, using the patients to express fear and anger. The dislike of violence which had led them to be c.o.s to begin with reduced the likelihood of their abusing patients. Habits of courtesy and kindness, learned in middle-class homes and schools as a matter of course, were invaluable on the ward, where patients fought to hold on to any scrap of individuality they could muster.

Patients were abused in many ways at Sykesville. Many attendants abused their patients verbally as a matter of course; scolding them, mocking them, or calling them names whenever they were intransigent. Others used the patients constantly to mop or polish the floors, or help with meals, a form of slave labor which was accepted as normal, even good for the patients in those days. Physical abuse ranged from snapping ones fingers in the patient's face, pushing or shoving roughly, using undue force to subdue the recalcitrant, to actual blows. If the doctors knew which attendants were abusive, they rarely reacted; it would rock the already shaky boat.

Throughout the war the hospital faced an ever increasing shortage of attendants as war industry drew off any able-bodied men and women. Sometimes they were forced to hire temporary help from any source they could find. Drifters, alcoholics, former felons, even former patients came to fill in for a few days or a week. Among the men particularly there were violent individuals who left a trail of abused patients in their wake. If such a person was discovered he or she would be fired, and there might be staff discussion about how to supervise more thoroughly. But it was meaningless talk. Who was to do the supervision? Meanwhile the whole staff became increasingly appreciative of the c.o.s and the hospital administrator told Ralph he would take all the c.o.s who could be sent to Sykesville.

While all conscientious objectors were committed in varying degrees to the concept that love was a more powerful force than violence, few in those days knew much about nonviolent theory.

Gandhi was at work in India but he was far more obscure than he has become, and of course the use of nonviolence in the struggle for racial justice was far in the future. Allen's fellow c.o.s on South I-A did not talk much about nonviolence, nor did they deliberately decide that they would use it on the ward, but they came to recognize in time that their use of nonviolent methods was what was making the difference.

Nonviolence does not always work, in the sense that it does not mean that its practitioners do not themselves sometimes get hurt, even killed. It is better to accept suffering than inflict it on others is the basic nonviolent theory. Allen's worst moment on South I-A came after a morning of shock treatments. Bippus was a thin, strong, wiry man, who had come onto the ward talking about blood and death, and lashing out from time to time at the other patients and attendants. He was one of the few patients to be kept in a locked room, and he was given shock treatments three times a week. It was at the end of a lunch period, when only Allen and Sam were on the ward, that Allen went into the locked room to give Bippus his lunch.

Bippus, having just come out of the confusion of shock was crouched in a corner, looking wild. "I want blood," he muttered, when he saw Allen.

"Come along, Bippus, eat your lunch," Allen cajoled.

Previously Bippus had complied, but this time he shot forward, and before Allen quite knew what was happening, had him by the throat, on his back, on the floor of the room. Allen struggled to free himself, but Bippus had the advantage of surprise, and was able to control Allen by tightening his grip. Allen could scarcely make a sound, and what noise the struggle produced did not reach Sam, who was at the other end of the ward in the dayroom, supervising lunch. For a while Allen didn't know how it was going to end. Bippus increased the pressure on his windpipe, and he began to see blackness before his eyes. Finally, making a desperate lunge with his whole body, he was able to throw the two of them against the heavy open door so that it crashed against the wall and got Sam's attention. Sam came running, pried Bippus's fingers from

Allen's windpipe, waited until Allen was on his feet, then called for extra help. It took three men to get Bippus back into his room, and he continued to scream in a state of wild excitement until he was given a needle of sedative. The next morning, his name was once more back on the shock list.

Allen, being tall and strong, was often called up to the women's violent ward to help drag some particularly resistant patient to the shock treatment room. I was working on South II-A the day he and Sam came to help us move a very fat, very agitated woman, who clung, stark naked to the bare springs of a metal cot. "I'm an honorable Jewish mother! I'm an honorable Jewish mother!" she shouted. Some of the attendants snickered, but I felt sick. Long after that morning I remembered the woman and the desperate appeal for dignity in her eyes.

Fortunately for us there was a young psychiatrist assigned to the admissions building who felt as we did about the shock treatments. Matthew was tall and lean, only a few years older than we were. He was in training to be an analyst and had already had far more psychiatric training than the other doctors at Sykesville, but he sometimes had a hard time articulating his hypotheses in staff meeting and was easily put off by the scorn of his superiors. Yet he persisted in raising difficult questions. What difference did it make whether we classify a man or woman as paranoid or schizophrenic? What did that have to do with what was going on inside him? What was she trying to tell us by her behavior? What were we doing to meet her real needs? Did we really believe that disturbed behavior had no meaning? Couldn't we try to understand that a person tried to save his or her self through symptoms, just as a person ran a fever to throw off infection? Why couldn't we, just this one time, try to find out what was going on? Why must we subject the person to the indiscriminate torture of shock?

But Matthew lost, time after time, even with those patients assigned to his care. Grimly he would go with the attendants to the shock room, and tightlipped, throw the switch.

Common abhorrence of shock treatment, and a whole administrative structure that seemed more intent on keeping the floors waxed, the patients quiet, the uniforms starched, the proper entries made on the charts, than in trying to minister or to cure, drew us closer to Matthew. He and his pretty wife, Liz, became our friends, though this friendship bothered Matthew's fellow physicians and made us further estranged from our more conventional unit comrades. We spent hours in his apartment playing games, looking at his most recent photographs, or just chatting. After a few months Matthew offered to give interested attendants from the unit a course on interpersonal relations, based on his studies under psychiatristHarry Stack Sullivan.

"The most important question a person has to answer is where does he leave off and the rest of the world begin," Matthew was fond of quoting Sullivan. Gradually, through his eyes, we began to see the patients as men and women fighting for health and wholeness through their very symptoms. By trying to suppress those symptoms by treating them all alike, the hospital was answering their cries for help with brutal disregard. "Learn to conform, learn to live here so as not to upset our routines, learn to be a good worker, and we offer you security and safety," the hospital said. "Cooperate, and we will make you safe from yourself." The victims of this policy were the gray men and women on either hill, while those with an ounce of fight left were kept at Hubner and punished with shock treatment.

And yet Matthew was part of the system and, like the very young man he was, better able to formulate his rebellion than his concept of alternatives. Like us, he wanted the hospital to be run more humanely and therapeutically. Like us, he missed the point that perhaps the great impersonal hospital itself was the problem, more of a social ill than the sickness it had been established to cure. Matthew, in fact, went on to a career in mental hospital administration, reforming the very institution he once so passionately wanted to escape. But we owed him much for opening our eyes to think of process, not product, and to trust those instincts which told us that torturing our fellow human beings in the name of treatment could not be right.

There were three regular doctors in addition to Matthew at the

Hubner Building; Dr. Wiseman, the clinical director; and Dr. Futterman and Dr. Venig both Austrian refugees.

Dr. Wiseman was the oldest son in a Jewish family which had come to Maryland from Russia thirty years earlier. I felt warmer toward him when I saw his mother, a little old woman with a lopsided twist of gray hair on the top of her head and eyes gleaming with pride over her doctor son. The pride was tainted however. Melvin had married a shicksa, and the little grandchildren whom the old mama came to see were going to a Methodist Sunday School.

I never quite understood Melvin Wiseman, but after a while it seemed to me that he was burning with a need to get away from all that had been painful to him as a child; to become rich and powerful, to be accepted by the middle-class American society, the white Protestant society, which had rejected his parents. His ease of manner, his apparent warmth with patients and with colleagues, cost him nothing, and were attitudes he slipped into with the same lack of effort as he slipped into his white jacket.

After I became a social worker he liked to chat with me, to draw me out about Allen and myself, but he never revealed much of his personal life. I was left to puzzle over certain incongruities; why, with his ambition, had he chosen the state mental hospital, surely the less well paid and less status conferring choice he might have made after internship? And why, if he wanted to marry a Protestant, had he chosen such a meek seeming small town girl as Becky?

We never became friends with the Wisemans, but we saw enough of them to observe that Melvin completely dominated his pale wife. She was always flurried and slightly breathless when we saw them together, trying to keep up with his pace, his demands; and she never spoke except to answer a direct question in his presence. Rumors spread through our gossipy little colony that he used her for his guinea pig as he tried to master new techniques of psychiatry. She was his subject when he studied hypnosis, it was said. There was other talk, even less pleasant, that hung about them like smoke. I had the feeling at times of something not quite right behind Wiseman's bland exterior.

And yet, the patients loved him. He cared little about them, I felt; his chief interest was in slapping a diagnosis upon them that permitted him to give them the maximum number of shock treatments, but he had a certain earthy warmth, a heartiness to which these sick and frightened men and women clung. Returning patients asked for him, begged that he be assigned to them, pushed others aside to greet him on the wards, smiled at him as he threw the electro shock switch. How could they confuse the dross of his spurious kindness for the gold of real concern, I asked Allen at night? Or was the fault in my eyes, for thinking so ill of him?

Matthew in contrast, for all his worrying over his patients, his deep concern for their treatment, his opposition to shock treatment, was unpopular with the patients. He lacked the common touch and seemed cold and haughty to many. Interviewing patients and their families on arrival, he never helped when a patient or a relative groped for a word or misunderstood a question. The impression one got was that he preferred to let them flounder through the interview in their own way, making their own mistakes. This was in fact part of his conception of a therapeutic relationship. In analysis himself at the time, and involved in several control analytic therapeutic relationships, he was trying to give the patient a chance to confront his own problems in his own manner. The theory may have been right, but in practice it came out as a form of personal withdrawal, and it turned the interview into a cold and awkward experience.

In time we got to know Matthew and Liz pretty well. And yet in his private life there were mysteries we never quit penetrated. Matthew was the son of a wealthy and prominent family. His father was a surgeon and one brother a physiologist; neither of them were attracted to psychiatry and rather looked down their noses at Matthew's choice. Did this bother him? And if not why did he choose to tell us? He found his own analysis a grim experience, and seemed abstracted and lonely much of the time. He was fortunate in his wife; Liz being a sweet, warm., healthy person, and they had two wonderful little girls. Otherwise, he might have found Sykesville unbearable.

The two refugee doctors from Vienna at least did not have to ask themselves why they were at Sykesville. They were there because it was the only place in the United States where they could find jobs while they went through the long laborious process of acquiring citizenship, and passing various medical boards. Neither had had any particular acquaintance with psychiatry in Vienna, and had perhaps rather opposed the discipline, but here ironically it represented the one field open the them.

Of the two, Dr. Futterman accepted the demands of fate with better grace. He was a quiet, unassuming man who had been a general practitioner in Europe, and he had a charming and serene wife whom he adored. One thought of a quiet, pleasant life for them: the opera in season, weekends in the mountains, a tiny perfect backyard garden. Instead, they had barely escaped concentration camp and were thrown into a culture entirely alien to everything they had ever cared about. Only a saving urbanity and humor stood between them and despair.

At the hospital, Dr. Futterman was quiet, conscientious, and interested in his patients, but he suffered tremendously from language and culture barriers. Often when he was talking to a patient he would turn to the attendant with half humorous despair and ask her to translate or explain. The experience of the Hitler years had damaged his faith in himself, I came to believe; beneath his pleasant facade he believed in very little, least of all his capacity to heal.

Dr. Vendig had been through much the same experience, getting out of Austria just in time, but she had come out quite differently; bitter, suspicious, scrappy. She was so quick to suspect a slight that we wondered if she might be becoming paranoid, and her fear of the patients was palpable whenever she came onto the ward. As with the attendants, this fear communicated itself to the patients and created more anxiety and more acting out. The wards were always in turmoil when Dr. Vendig was on them.

We speculated endlessly about Dr. Vendig. She was both young and pretty, with blue eyes, curly brown hair, and an opulent but trim figure, but her fear of the patients was only matched by her fear of men. She froze at the slightest advance, and since she was distant with women also, she lived a nun's life. Yet word spread that her underclothes, washed by the convalescent patient assigned to her apartment, were of pure silk and lace, and that she retired at night in a robe of satin trimmed with feathers. This kind of complete lack of privacy was part of the high pressured community in which we lived. What, we asked, was one to make of this voluptuousness beneath the starched white jacket and frozen manner?

In addition to these four, a fifth, Dr. Klein alternated her time between the Women's Group and Hubner. Dr. Klein was a refugee also, but there the resemblance between her and Dr. Vendig ended. Wise, kind, self-contained and quiet, she emanated an air of strength and sanity whenever she came down to give us a hand. We saw her infrequently, and rarely heard her, but unless pressed for an opinion she did not speak up in staff meeting. Years later however, it was her few words of wisdom I remembered.

We never knew much about Dr. Klein. She was married to a lawyer, who shared an apartment at the hospital with her, and commuted into the city each day, and the two had many interests that kept them to themselves at night. I heard (but it was second hand) that she belonged to a well-to-do Jewish family converted to Christianity in Berlin, and that the experience of Hitlerism had turned her back to her grandparents' religion in search of a sense of identity. Whatever her secret, she seemed like a whole person, a rarity at Sykesville.

The medical staff at Hubner was new to the hospital. Dr. Wiseman, who had been there the longest, had preceded our arrival by only five years; the rest arrived when we did or shortly thereafter. Medical turnover was rapid in a state mental hospital; those who could possibly move on did so as quickly as possible. The doctors at Men's Group, Women's Group, and the Epileptic Colony on the other hand had been at Sykesville for many years, and with each one of the five there proved to be some reason that kept them there. One was himself an alcoholic; another had a drug addicted wife; another preferred men at a time when society's attitudes toward homosexuals was even more vicious and punishing than today. The women doctors seemed to have fewer problems, but they ran their Group like a navy ship, and one sensed that here was an outlet for a driving need to control.

Sykesville, in fact, seemed something like a ship; with the doctors the officers, the attendants the crew, and the patients, the passengers, all sailing through rough seas toward an unknown destination. Although it was possible to get away from the hospital at infrequent intervals, the life of the hospital became the most compelling reality we knew, dominating our thinking and our feelings throughout our waking hours, and through dreams at night. So powerful was its influence, that one could understand how both patients and long-term staff became institutionalized. Many years later, when states began to dismantle their mental hospitals and deinstitutionalize the care of mental patients, we applauded, although the wholesale manner in which this was done left much to be desired.

It was a strange environment in which to try to work out some of the intricacies of our new marriage, to deal with the complexities of being conscientious objectors during a war popular with the vast majority of our fellow citizens, to try to understand what we meant by nonviolence, far from our Hindu guru Dr. Chatterjee, or other members of our little Ahimsa group. The very dailiness of life on the wards with its constant demands made it hard to take time to take stock of ourselves and our beliefs. But we were very young, and the urge to grow and develop was strong, no matter what our surroundings. For all its horrors, Sykesville formed a significant part of our lives, and some of the friendships we made there have lasted a lifetime.

Chapter V

I HAD ENDURED THE LONG DAYS ON THE WARDS because I knew that soon I would be transferred to the social services department. Whenever I saw the social workers, they were sitting at desks, typing or dictating records, wearing office clothes with sometimes a white smock. Occasionally they looked a bit harried, but from the point of view of the attendant who must be on her feet for twelve hours at a time, and whose uniform was frequently smeared and rumpled as a result of combat with patients over meals or baths, their status looked heavenly. I began to live for the day of my transfer.

In the middle of August that transfer finally came through. We spent a few vacation days at a cottage owned by Allen's aunt on a lake in the Pocono mountains visiting his parents and sister, and enjoying the misty coolness and the silence after the din of Sykesville days. We swam in the lake, sailed on it, and took long walks through the pine forests and along the river below the dam, brushing against sweet smelling fern. It felt unreal to be there, as though our place was back in the heat and the turmoil of the hospital, but it also felt wonderful to have escaped briefly into a scene from our former life. At night we went out to view the stars, which seemed brighter and closer than in Maryland, then slept heavily until long after the sun rose. All too soon it was time to return to Sykesville in order for me to take up my new duties as admissions officer.

I started in Admissions on a Monday morning. I had previously been shown my new office, but this was my first opportunity to examine it at leisure. Admissions consisted actually of two rooms; a small waiting room off the main hall, and behind it an office with two desks. Mine was the smaller desk in a corner, facing the wall. A larger, empty desk sat by the window. This was occupied by the doctor when it was time for him to take part in the admissions procedure.

Since admissions was the first contact between the patient, his family, and the hospital, some small effort had been made to make the office attractive. Someone had hung drapes at the windows, a few muddy watercolors on the walls, and there was even a little yellow vase for flowers on my desk. On the other hand, we were stuck with the same dark ceramic tile and buff paint as the rest of Hubner Building. Light penetrated only sparsely from the courtyard, and the institutional smell of Klomine penetrated even here. It was not a cheerful or homey office, and few patients were deceived about its true nature.

One of the social workers was the wife of a unit member and friend of mine, and it was she who spent the first morning with me, explaining my new duties. Persons to be admitted were brought to the hospital by the family, by the police, or by attendants from other hospitals, making a transfer. Whenever possible, appointments for admissions were made in advance, and only two or three admissions scheduled for a day. Over weekends however the rate tended to go up, as emergencies occurred and discharged patients had to be readmitted.

Maryland was at this time already enjoying a well-earned reputation as a progressive state in the field of mental health. Unlike most states, it did not require court proceedings for admission to a mental hospital, except in the case of the criminally insane. Instead, admission papers were signed by the family, or occasionally by the patient himself, with the authority for commitment buttressed by the opinions of two independent psychiatrists. This made for less institutional control over patients and more flexibility; families could remove patients against medical advice if they wished, or bring them back again; patients could under certain circumstances sign themselves out.

The social service department placed great stress on involving the family in the admission procedure. We were urged to give relatives a sense of participation in the admission, encouraging them to keep in touch with the patient and to plan for a future beyond the hospital. If relatives did not come along with the patient at the time of admission, we insisted that they come shortly thereafter to give us a case history, and to learn about the hospital and its procedures and plans.

This working with the families was to be my principal job as admissions social worker, I was told. When the patient and his or her relatives first arrived I was to welcome them, fill out a few preliminary details on the admission form, and reassure them as best I could before calling the doctor. After the doctor's admission interview was completed, I was to talk further with the relatives, telling them about the hospital, and making an appointment for them to come back for an admission's interview of their own; or, if it were more convenient, conducting the interview on the spot.

One object of the admissions interview, with either the patient or his relatives, or both was to obtain a case history. This case history in turn was used in staff conferences to arrive at a diagnosis of the patient's condition and prescribe treatment. The case histories which the social worker wrote following her admission interview followed a form of sorts . . ."early childhood," "education," "vocational history," "onset of illness," "onset of present episode," but they tended to be long, rambling, and inclusive. The head of the social service department, Matilda Van Dusen, was determined that her workers were to demonstrate that they had a role of equal stature to the doctors. One way to prove this was to present powerful and dramatic case histories to the diagnostic staff meetings. This, I discovered later, was one reason Mrs. Van Dusen had been so eager to have a writer in the admissions department. I threw myself into the case histories with enthusiasm, and mine were the longest, the most involved, the most dramatic in the hospital's recent history, I was told. In fact, as I began to learn, it was possible for me to influence the diagnosis of the patient by stressing one line of questioning when interviewing the relatives, or pursuing my own hypothesis in my interview and subsequent write-up. I was never tempted to use this power mischievously, but I do remember moments of secret dismay when my best schizophrenics turned out on medical examination to be paretics in advantaged stages of syphilis.

To record these long case histories I had a dictating machine with wax cylinders. Every afternoon I gathered up four or five of these cylinders and took them to a secretary in the front office who would transcribe them and return them to me, shaven and ready for a fresh interview. Occasionally mixups occurred; cylinders were shaved before they had been transcribed, or I had failed to press the button properly and took to the office an uncut cylinder.

Unfortunately my secretary and I were never able to straighten these matters out, since she had taken some sort of vow never to speak to a conscientious objector or his wife. Her own husband was overseas in the army, and this silence was for her an act of faithfulness and patriotism. We managed somehow; I learned to speak to her despite her stony reception; and she sometimes wrote me notes or asked someone else in the office to ask me something. It did not, however, make for a very pleasant relationship. My office was far away from the rest of the social service department, which was on the bottom floor of the building in another wing, and I was isolated from my friends on the wards. I came to depend upon the doctors for company.

That first morning, my friend Helen showed me how to fill in the admissions form, how to work the dictating machine, introduced me to the stony faced secretary, and gave me a jumbled but enthusiastic picture of my role and its importance to the hospital. Like all the social workers at Sykesville, she was an enthusiastic advocate of Matilda's ideas, based as I learned later on the theories Dr. Otto Rank had developed at the Pennsylvania School of Social Work. These theories made much of the use of time. Because admissions was a crisis in the lives of both patients and relatives, she said, it could be a time of great growth. We could use the hour to help relatives get rid of the enormous burden of guilt which they brought with them, and assist them in unmasking the rejection and hostility under that guilt. Only when these feelings were in the open could the relative grow toward realistic planning for the future.

It sounded great. I accepted the theory enthusiastically, and believed myself to be operating on the basis of it for many months. Only much later did I begin to question the relationship between these fine ideals of growth and the locked wards and shock treatment and the long, long line of shuffling shadows on the hill. Helen left finally for other duties. I read through the case histories she had left for me, wondering if I would know when to write "disoriented" or "hyperkinetic" in the right places. I sharpened pencils, looked through the desk, reviewed the appointments for later in the week which preceding social workers had made for me. Lunchtime came, and still no patients arrived.

"I'll have to take my typewriter so I have something to do in the intervals," I told Allen while we ate together in the attendant's dining room. Because of my new status I could have eaten in the smaller alcove set off for social workers and administrative personnel, but of course I wanted to be with Allen.

"I don't believe I'd do that. It can get a little exciting in there at times," Allen said.

Because of his size, Allen was frequently called to the admissions office when a particularly obstreperous patient had to be taken back to the wards. I shivered slightly, realizing that the sense of physical danger, which I had hoped to leave behind me when I left ward duty, was to be with me still.

Shortly after lunch I had my first admission. Two police officers appeared in my anteroom, holding between them a highly excited man of middle years shouting stridently and incoherently. To my horror the officers undid the man's handcuffs and pushed him gently toward my little inner office, themselves standing way back. I had the impression they were afraid of him. So was I.

" Please sit down," I said to the man, trying to summon my best professional manner. "I have a few questions to ask you if I may?"

"At your service, my dear young lady," he said grandly.

"First of all, please, your name?"

"My dear, cannot you recognize me? I am the risen Lord."

I picked up the inner phone and called the doctor on duty. "We are ready for you," I said, trying to keep a quaver out of my voice.

> "The woman saith unto him, I know that Messiah cometh, which is called Christ; when he is come he will tell us all things," the man quoted. "That's from John, young lady. And I said to those who brought me hence, why bringeth thou me thither . . ."

The doctor on duty strode into the office. It was Dr. Wiseman. "Where are the admission papers?" he asked me.

I apologized and went out into the anteroom. The police officers had vanished, and in their place was a worn looking middle-aged woman, clutching the precious documents in her hand. I asked her for them, and took them to the doctor who was asking routine questions to determine the patient's orientation. What day of the week was this? What month? What year? Who was president?

"Year one of our risen Lord," the patient said triumphantly. He arose and started pacing the small office. Dr. Wiseman sighed and called the admissions ward to bring two attendants.

"What place is this?" the patient asked suddenly, "What are you doing to me?.

"This is a hospital," Dr. Wiseman explained. "You are here to get rested. Try saying Methodist-Episcopal."

"I need no hospital," the man said. "I need a hillside," He looked about wildly. I was immensely relieved to see Allen and Sam in the doorway.

"What's his name?" Allen asked Dr. Wiseman.

Dr. Wiseman glanced at the papers. "He's the reverend William Oliver," he said.

"Come with us now sir," Allen said cordially.

"I am He who is called to come after ye," the minister said. He rose however, and went docilely enough with Allen.

Dr. Wiseman got up, sighed, and dropped the admissions form on my desk.

"See what you can get from the wife," he said. "And ask her to sign this."

He left, and I went into the anteroom to look for Mrs. Oliver. She was sitting on the same bench where I had seen her before, but she looked somehow softened and crumpled. I noticed that she twisted a handkerchief between her fingers, and that her eyes were red.

"If you'll just come in here for a few moments, Mrs. Oliver," I said. I suddenly felt the presumption of my situation; that I at twenty-three was supposed to help and comfort this middle-aged grief-stricken woman, and wring from her the story of her troubles.

To my surprise, however, Mrs. Oliver dabbed at her eyes, then brightened, smiled, and began eagerly to answer my questions. I saw she took no note of my age; I was officialdom, and she was pulling the shreds of her dignity firmly around her in order to deal with the official. We sailed easily through the questions on the admission sheet and began on the case history. Her husband had no previous episode of mental illness, nor any illnesses or troubles to speak of. Mrs. Oliver had met Bill Oliver when he was in seminary. Before that he had been in the navy. She knew little of his infancy and childhood, beyond the fact of his being born and brought up on a farm in West Virginia.

Had there been any history of mental illness in the family? Mrs. Oliver wasn't sure. But Bill had certainly never been ill a day in his life that she knew of. It was she who had been laid low with flebitus after the birth of their second child, and had been troubled by her gall bladder. They had moved several times from church to church, Bill liking things to be done just so in his parish, but altogether it had been a serene life until recently.

"He began to change about three months ago," she said, sitting up, her eyes sparkling with excitement. "He started to talk loudly and use words that he had never used before." She paused and saw the question in my eyes. "Dirty words, like fuck and shit and words like that," she said primly. "He began to bother me a lot, in that way, you know, and to sing songs he had learned in the navy. They noticed at church that he was acting a little strangely, and they wanted him to take a vacation. But he only wanted to stay around the house, and he kept getting more and more excited.

"Last Saturday was the worst. He got the idea we ought to house-clean. 'Bill, I said, I housecleaned just this past Thursday.' But no, nothing for it but to get out the vacuum cleaner. Then he took off all his clothes, and he made me take off all my clothes, and he chased me around the house with that vacuum cleaner." She shook her head as though in disbelief. "I got kind of scared, and I ran outdoors, even with nothing on, and he came after me and chased me down the street. Finally, someone saw us and called the cops, and they came and got him, and a neighbor gave me a coat to cover myself with, and they held him in the county jail until it was time to bring him here."

"How terrible for you," I said. I was scribbling down her story, but mystified by this sudden change in middle life. I turned the pages of the admissions papers that Dr. Wiseman had given me. "Waserman positive," I saw. "Diagnosis: possible paresis." That tour in the navy, I thought, and the spirochetes waiting like a time bomb under the surface of the placid pastoral life.

"O, it was terrible, "Mrs. Oliver agreed. "My sister said, 'Ada, I don't know how you stood it. You with your nerves in the condition they are at your time of life.'"

Mrs. Oliver dabbed at her eyes again, but I saw that her pity and grief were for herself. I swallowed hard and then in as neutral tone of voice as I could summon I began to tell her about the hospital, the visiting rules, the new concept for quick treatment and early recovery. If it were really paresis I knew this was prob-ably false. At that time they could halt the spread of the disease by malaria treatment, but the brain and possibly the spinal col-umn might be already riddled by the spirochetes.

Mrs. Oliver, however, evidently had no suspicions about the nature of her husband's disease. She said piously that she hoped indeed they could do something for poor Bill, and meanwhile she intended to get a good rest, and see her own doctor immediately. She patted her eyes again, got up, thanked me, and left.

I sat back and thought over the interview. I had certainly not achieved the dramatic and emotional breakthrough which Matilda Van Dusen thought each such occasion would produce. On the other hand, I had gotten the information which the hospital needed, and given the poor woman the small comfort of a bland piece of business as usual. I didn't think I had done badly, and I suspected it was going to be an exciting job.

The admissions office was the portal to the hospital. Through my door came, week after week, month after month, every specimen of deranged humanity that populated the huge warehouse buildings on the hill. At first each case seemed new, but after a while they fell into a pattern and I learned to recognize the familiar plots, repeated over and over in a weary round of human tragedy.

There were the alcoholics, brought in by the police, or by members of Alcoholics Anonymous, or occasionally a long-suffering spouse. Sometimes they came into my office in the full bloom of *delirium tremens,* and saw little mice scampering up and down the walls behind me, but more often they were depressed, morose, often believing they were suffering from some loathsome and fatal disease. Their stories had a sameness, the never quite succeeding at anything, the drinking and the drying up, the noble resolves and then the return to alcohol.

There were the depressed, many of them in middle age, whom we dubbed in our rage for labels as involutional melancholies. Here the patterns were less clear, often a life of apparent adjustment, sliding into deep depressions in the fifties and sixties. Many of these men and women were the pictures of despondency, but some cloaked their desperation in an overactive gaiety. The doctors called these agitated depressives and ordered massive shock therapy. Whether because or despite of the treatment, most of these depressions cleared up and the patients went home, but a few remained permanently in despair, and one or two committed suicide.

There were the senile, elderly men and women brought in in states of confusion and fright such as I had come to know on the infirmary ward. Here in the admissions office I saw the relatives that brought them; the gray-faced middle-aged woman who had cared for her mother until she finally gave up, in a paroxysm of guilt and anger; the rejecting daughter-in-law; the over solicitous niece, the elderly spouse or sibling, seeming almost as befuddled as the patient. With all these relatives I devoted myself to reassurance; for how after all in practical terms could a family continue to deal with a mother who got up and wandered about the house lighting candles in the middle of the night; or a grandfather who dirtied his bed and feared to tell? There were far less community resources for such people than there are today.

And yet, and yet . . . one couldn't help feeling that in an earlier, simpler time there would have been a place by the fireside for many of these old people, and that the household might have been richer for the constant stream of memories which even the most confused brought forth.

That the hospital was seen, among other things, as a sort of dumping ground for society, for the lonely old man or woman, for the slightly feeble-minded aunt, or the unwanted child with epilepsy, for any piece of human flotsam and jetsam which could not be pawned off elsewhere, became increasingly clear to me. We made space for the desperately ill individual, and by a sort of horrid extension of Gresham's law, we filled up every bed with hundreds and hundreds of men and women whose sickness was chiefly that they made social problems for their family or for society.

Years later, I heard the story of a refugee from Eastern Europe who came to this country seeking lost relatives, was unable to make herself understood to anyone, became distraught, and was placed in the nearest state mental hospital, where she spent twenty-seven years. She was only discovered and released when a social worker who spoke her language happened to interview her and discovered that she was perfectly sane. I don't think I helped to admit such a person to Sykesville, but I wonder.

There were many whose mental illness had a physical basis. In time I learned the neurological signs; the fixed stare and slurred speech of the paretic; the mask-like face and muscular rigidity of the person suffering from post encephalitic syndrome. We admitted many epileptics, and not infrequently the trauma of admission produced a grand mal attack right on the floor of my office; I learned how to cope but I was always frightened by a seizure. And we even got some young adults suffering from Down's syndrome who had developed emotional problems as a result of living with anxious parents.

I think particularly of Fruitcake, so named for his love of everything sweet and his constant mumble, "cookies, candies, fruitcake." Fruitcake's mother had been forty when she had him, and had evidently never accepted his limitations; his short life had been a hell of training, training, training, and underlying rejection. Fruitcake dealt with this as best he knew how by deciding he was superman. Once in a while he would suddenly go wild, and attempt to climb the walls, to show that he could walk upside down, like his hero. Because of these occasional fits he was assigned to the violent ward, where he became a pet of the attendants and patients alike. Like many in his circumstance, he seemed to have a special talent for loving relationships.

The most interesting to me were the true psychotics, the manic-depressives and the schizophrenics. The manics were exciting, bringing into the office the frenzied gaiety of their temporary liberation from the bonds of super ego, cracking jokes, talking in rhymes, and occasionally amusing us with their delusions. We did indeed admit both a Napoleon and a Mary Queen of Scots.

Soon, however, one began to recognize the despair and self-accusation behind the elation; especially as patients hospitalized in the manic state fell into deep depressions on the ward. Also, sometimes the manic excitement had reached the state of frenzy before the man or the woman was brought to us, and then there indeed was violence in my little office. I remember one heavy set woman who jerked the curtains from the window and tried to tear down the Venetian blinds. I didn't quite run away from her, but I stepped to my office door and waited anxiously for the attendants to arrive.

But of all the sad procession that came through my office door, the saddest, the most appealing, the most baffling to me were the schizophrenics. Many were young, in their late teens or early twenties, and I knew from reading hospital records how likely it was that the disease would reoccur and reoccur, until finally all stretches of normalcy would be lost, and the patient would become one of our shuffling shadows on the hill. I knew too, from personal experience what lay ahead of them on the wards; the bedlam of the Disturbed Ward, the incomprehensible shock treatments, the anger that seemed to motivate many of the attendants. I could never quite feel my way into the inner world of the schizophrenic--a creature of ups and downs, it was easier for me to imagine myself into the shoes of the manic-depressive-- but I could guess at the terrible confusion of two worlds making competing demands.

Chestnut Lodge, the private mental hospital where Dr. Frieda von Reichman was said to be having success with pyschotherapy for schizophrenics, was not far from Sykesville, and our favorite psychiatrist, Matthew, was doing his control analysis there. Later we would read the book "I Never Promised You a Rose Garden," based on this therapy, and try to believe that there was hope at least for the few privileged enough to afford private treatment. But hope was a commodity in short supply at Sykesville.

Schizophrenics had one virtue from my point of view; they made wonderful subjects for my case histories. The stories were inevitably long and full of drama, and it seemed easy to follow clues to the development of the illness in early childhood. Many of the young schizophrenics were accompanied by their mothers. We were taught that these mothers were peculiarly unable to see their sick child as a person apart from themselves, and many of the women I interviewed seemed to bear this out. To the question: "When was the child trained to the pot?" the mother would answer. "Oh, I was the sort of mother who didn't allow anything dirty around her children." Or if I asked a question about weaning, it would be answered by a diatribe against the way the mother had been treated by the nurses in the hospital.

Perhaps because I was young I identified closely with the young schizophrenics, and was angry at the mothers and to a lesser extent the fathers, who could use a child subconsciously for their own psychological ends. Through the courses which Matthew arranged for us to take, we were learning a little more about interpersonal relations, and I was beginning to understand how a family could be hooked up together like some Rube Goldberg machine, with the sick member actually helping the rest of the family to work. I knew my role as a social worker was not to take sides, but to hear the mother of a baffled eighteen-year-old girl spend her time with me concentrating on self justification was sometimes more than I could bear. I wanted very badly to tell them where I thought their fault lay, and sometimes in my priggishness, I came as close as I dared to saying it in veiled language.

Altogether, the relatives were as disheartening to me as the patients themselves. In a few I saw genuine love and grief to which I could relate, but the vast majority seemed to me more concerned about themselves, their pride and self image, and yes, even in this dreadful hour, the impression they were making on me, than they cared about the loved one they had just brought to the hospital. I sometimes had great difficulty steering the conversation back to the patient and his symptoms. Many seemed to need to use the hour to justify themselves. When I talked about hospital procedures, relatives often looked blank, and when I suggested it that was not too soon to begin to plan for the patient's return from the hospital, I was often met with a flash of consternation, as though bringing the person here was the final solution to some dreadful problem, and there was to be no future.

Perhaps the relatives were in shock; and this was a natural reaction. Newspaper reporters say that when they visit a home which has just experienced a death there is often the same sort of inappropriate response; bereaved mothers and fathers smile for the camera and are eager to tell their side of the story with emphasis on *their* shock, *their* state of health, and so forth. Only later does true grieving begin. I was young and intolerant when I began work at Sykesville, however, and I could not quite forgive this initial lack of involvement, especially, I suppose, since it seemed to echo the detachment I felt in myself.

One day several months after I started to work in admissions, a nice looking man in his late thirties was brought in on a stretcher, with his wrists bandaged, having attempted suicide several nights before. With him was his wife, a tall, intelligent, serious-looking woman with short dark hair, and another man, also tall, distinguished, with wavy gray hair. The patient was confined to the stretcher and the attendants wheeled it into my little office. The man and the woman came too. Since we were desperately crowded I inquired politely if the man was also a relative.

"No, he's John's best friend," the wife said.

"That's right," the patient said sarcastically, "the best friend a man ever had."

I filled out the admissions sheet, rang for the doctors and sat through his short admissions interview, which did little to enlighten me. Afterwards the best friend left to wait outside in the car, and the wife, Ruth, stayed to give me the case history.

Her husband, she told me, was a master in a private boy's school. Early in their marriage they had become close friends with another master and his wife, and after a few months the intimacy ripened into a close relationship between herself and the other man, Stewart. Just as things were reaching a climax, however, Stewart and his wife had moved away, to become headmaster at another boys school, and she and John had been left to lead a quiet, contented life with their three children.

But then, eighteen months ago, Stewart had looked them up and invited John to come and teach in his school and John, for a variety of reasons, had accepted. The friendship between the two couples was immediately once more intense, and the sexual attraction between herself and Stewart was reborn. This time they entered into a physical relationship as well, though Ruth was as frigid with her lover as she had been with her husband, she told me. It was the discovery of this relationship a few days ago that had precipitated John's suicide attempt.

All this time, as the tale of woe tumbled out, I kept trying to ask the appropriate questions about the patient: anything significant about John's childhood? Sense of accomplishment in his job? Closeness with his children? Involved in other interpersonal or civic relationships? Previous episodes of despondency? And all these questions Ruth brushed aside.

In desperation, I tried a direct approach. "I want to talk with you about John, and his illness, and plans for his future." I told her.

She was equally direct. "I don't want to talk about that now. I want to know what I should do? Should I marry Stewart? Or stick with John? Who cares about me?"

"Maybe you ought to get some counseling help when you get home," I suggested. "Here our function is only to help in relation to the patients."

She sighed heavily and began in a dispirited fashion to try to answer my questions. It was not a successful interview, and she left shortly thereafter, thoroughly depressed. I knew I had been technically true to the definition of my function which Matilda Van Dusen insisted upon, but I had a sneaking feeling that I might have helped the woman more if I hadn't been angry at her for her concentration on her own troubles, and her apparent disregard for the suffering of her distracted husband.

"I don't know," I told Allen that night, "the more I see of people in this light the less I am able to believe in the innate goodness of human beings."

"Maybe our civilization has taught people to repress so much they have learned to repress the good as well as the bad," Allen suggested.

"I don't see much repressed goodness breaking out here," I answered dispiritedly. "Today I had this self-involved woman in the morning, and in the afternoon, an eighty-year-old woman who kept hitching up her skirt to show her bare bottom in the admissions waiting room."

"We don't have to wait for the millennium to believe that war is barbaric," Allen pointed out. " We're not looking for a society without conflict, we're looking for more civilized ways to resolve conflict."

We were sliding, as we often did these days, into an old round-and- round discussion; knowing what we now did about human nature, was pacifism after all an impractical dream? Did we indeed really have a better way to stop Hitler?

It was I who most frequently raised the issue, I who needled and prodded Allen about his pacifism with increasing frequency.

The hostility of the regular hospital staff toward the c o.s bothered me far more than it bothered him. I wanted to answer back, and at the same time I wanted to be reassured that I was right. And the headlines from the war front bothered me too. Many of my friends from my New York childhood days were the wives of soldiers now, believing that force was the only way to stop Hitler and his atrocities. We did not know much about the concentration camps in those days, but we knew enough to be horrified. A distant cousin of my grandmother had written to her pleading for her help in escaping from Germany. I cared a great deal more than I often admitted to myself about how the war came out, and try as I might I could not imagine how it might have been fought nonviolently.

Allen was feeling disturbed about our situation too, but for different reasons. At the beginning of the draft he had intended to be a nonregistrant and go to jail rather than cooperate with the conscription system by becoming a registered c.o. Conscription he argued was one of the means which made war possible in the modern world. His family had influenced him against the nonregistrant position, and he had given way, hoping that in alternative service there would be an opportunity to prove the efficacy of nonviolence. Here at Sykesville he felt trapped, neither confronting conscription nor making a visible witness to an alternative way of life. I often tried to point out to him that the reaction of his patients to the respect he gave them was itself a witness. But Allen never thought in those terms. He seemed to take for granted his courtesy as much as his height, and to get no particular satisfaction from the respect he won.

So both restless and both guilty, but for different reasons, we talked often late into the night, trying to fit our new experiences with bedrock human emotions into our previous world view, and trying to decide whether it would be possible after all to spend the rest of the war at Sykesville, a debate which continued unresolved until VJ Day brought us to the end of the war. Still at the hospital.

Chapter VI

G oing to work in the social services department meant coming into the orbit of Matilda van Dusen. Matilda was a powerful figure, I sometimes thought the most powerful figure, at Sykesville. A tall and majestic woman, with a lovely head of wavy auburn hair piled on top of her head, Matilda ruled her social service department with the gracious manner of a queen. She expected and received loyalty from all of us who worked for her. In turn, she took a deep personal interest in our lives, and did what she could to make them happier and more pleasant despite the hospital setting.

We were her elite, her especially picked and trained troops, and she sent us forth daily to do battle with the medical department. It was part of the school of social work theory to which Matilda belonged to insist on the equal, but separate function of the social worker and the psychiatrist; we were not to fall into the familiar trap of regarding the doctor as God. It was also, I discovered, a part of Matilda's need to be recognized, a need never quite satisfied despite the homage she was paid on all sides.

At the time we came to Sykesville, Matilda was well known throughout the state for her pioneering work in placing patients in after care jobs or homes, and her social service department was the envy of most state mental hospitals on the East coast. She went further; she provided Sykesville with most of the theories with which the administration and doctors justified their procedures, whether shock treatment or locked wards, or the use of unpaid patient labor. At staff meetings she kept quiet unless called on, but through her social workers and through her close friendships with the doctors she was able to make a difference in the treatment afforded various patients. In time I came to see that the slanted case histories I wrote under her guidance served as tools in deciding which patients were sent where.

Matilda's power was the power of persuasion. She made one feel that she had great faith in one's power to grow, to change, to develop under her guidance, and one tried fervently to live up to these expectations. In our weekly supervision sessions, which she conducted as a form of therapy, she made me feel that I was an exceptionally talented and open young woman, and I blossomed dutifully for her as a result. I never remember tension between us; all was well until the very end, and then I was so appalled I could say nothing.

But like most of the other long-term staff members, Matilda had her Achilles heel. She had a young son who lived with her at the hospital, and went to a nearby school. We heard much about the son during our staff consultations in the social service department, but for a long time I was under the impression that there was no Mr. Van Dusen. Then I learned that he, too, ran drearily true to form for Sykesville spouses; he was an alcoholic and they lived apart because Matilda could no longer stand his drunken rages. Once or twice he came to the hospital to see her and his son, and I caught a glimpse of him, a tall, florid faced man with that over hearty assurance I had come to identify with the problem drinker. Matilda still loved him, and sometimes, when later in our relationship she spoke to me about him, she would cry, but for all her theories, all her psychiatric connections, she seemed to be quite unable to help him, or even to look to what responsibility she had in enabling his behavior.

Once, Matilda invited all her social workers and their spouses to her place on the Severn River for an afternoon of swimming. Otherwise, she did not socialize with us. We continued to spend occasional evenings with Matthew and Liz, but otherwise we passed most of our free time with other married couples of the unit, most of whom lived at the attendants' quarters in the Women's Group. Sam and Alice Durden, our best friends, lived here, and next door to them were Charles and Janet, Methodists from Minnesota of whom we became fond. In the same building on another floor lived the Thiermanns, Florence and Jim, who often took part in our late night bridge and poker games.

The rooms for attendants at the Women's Group were, if possible, more bleak than those at the Epileptic Colony. The walls were wainscotted with wood, covered with a brilliant orange varnish below, and dun colored, peeling paint above. The floors were carpeted with stained and cracked linoleum. Two narrow single beds, a tall wobbly dresser with drawers that stuck, and a chair, were the sole items of furniture, and a single naked bulb, hanging from the ceiling, lit each room. Sam and Alice had been promised a room in the new attendants' quarters across from Hubner, so they did not bother fixing up very much; aside from their personal belongings they left it stark.

And yet after a day or two on the wards, with five or six of us sitting around, smoking as we used to in those days, and perhaps sharing one precious bottle of beer, or a cup of coffee made on Alice's absolutely illicit hot plate, the Durden's room seemed warm with life and we hated to leave it and walk back to our own quarters. As a result we stayed and stayed and often dragged about the next day with puffy eyes.

Sam was a literature major from the University of Michigan, with a nice sense of humor. He often came out with something unexpectedly droll which amused him as well as the rest of us. When he thought we were getting a bit too gung-ho about psychiatry, Sam muttered, "Ah yes, my grandmother had bunions, and therefore was unable to give to my mother all the care and loving kindness she deserved, thereby insuring that I, the little bastard, would grow up with a fatally injured psyche." Or when something truly macabre happened (and at Sykesville the macabre happened everyday) he found a way to describe the event that somehow relieved the tension and made us all feel better. His story about the day he carried an amputated leg in a paper bag from the operating room to the front offices, and accidentally dropped the leg at the foot of a woman visitor, for example, was so popular that it became a hospital-wide legend.

Alice, a registered nurse, also had a good sense of humor and an infectious giggle. She was well-liked by other members of the nursing staff, and heard from them much of the hospital gossip which she related to us in the evenings. She liked to knit and crochet and whenever she was dummy in bridge she turned to her handiwork. Hers and Sam's seemed one of the happier marriages of the unit, and this happiness was probably one reason for their quarters exercising such an attraction to us all.

We played cards for pennies, and after a while we began to put our earnings into a common pot. The c.o.s were paid eleven dollars a month; we wives received something between $100 and $150 depending on our jobs. Since our room and board was provided this wasn't too bad in 1940 dollars, but we were always saving for a trip home, or to pay a debt, or to go to graduate school after the war, so we allowed ourselves to spend only a tiny fraction of our available cash each month. The pot went for common entertainment, a home-cooked meal on our day off; a trip to the movies, eventually a vacation in the Pocono mountains for us and the Durdens.

Card games were not our only diversion. We took many long cross country hikes, winter and summer, and on these we were often joined by Jim, the engineer from California, and sometimes Adam and Sally. Sometimes Adam came to work with Sam and Allen on South I-A. Sally worked in the front office down the hall from Admissions, along with my nonspeaking secretary, and her quick flash of smile was a help to me when I was forced to run the gauntlet of the hostility of the secretarial pool.

Several members of the unit had bicycles, and it was always possible to gather three or four and take a trip through the rolling Maryland countryside on our days off. Once we got as far as Fredericksburg. I was sore for days afterwards, but it was worth it. Getting away from the hospital with its labels, and achieving the anonymity of being simply a person always felt wonderful to me. I really hated being categorized as a c.o.'s wife. I wanted to be known as myself, although I had at this point in my life forgotten most of the feminism I had grown up with in Greenwich Village.

Besides, the bike rides brought back happy memories of summers I had spent with my best friend in Hampton Bays, Long Island. There, biking to the village to buy firecrackers for the Fourth of July, or sometimes to the bay bridge to crab, had been one of many pleasures. I did not have a bike of my own, but there were lots of bikes in the old stables on my friend's grandfather's estate, and one could help oneself to whichever fitted. Biking along the sandy side of the road, with the hot sun beating down, and the gulls mewing and wheeling overhead had been pure pleasure. If one got hot, there was always the promise of a swim in the surf in the afternoon to look forward too. If I squinched up my eyes, the rolling Maryland landscape was transformed into the flat Long Island terrain and I was twelve again.

In addition to biking we had other pleasures. During the hot summer months we searched for a place to swim. Once Matthew and Liz took us to a pool they belonged to and once or twice we ventured as far as the Chesapeake shore. There were tennis courts in the nearby town and we managed to play frequently on our days off. A bowling alley in the basement of the attendants' quarters gave us many happy evenings. And occasionally we would go to a nearby roller skating rink and rent skates, an extravagant treat paid for by the working wives.

Jim, the engineer, was a great folk dance enthusiast, and arranged for us many evenings of folk dancing, often to records, but occasionally to our own callers. Not all members of the unit came, the stricter Brethren being opposed to dancing, but it was fun and good exercise for the rest of us. In the winter we danced in a basement room of the attendants' quarters; in the summer, outdoors in a sort of natural dell which the hospital had outfitted with bright lights for evening events. Here the men of the unit often played baseball until dark. Here, too, we had our fellowship evenings on Sundays, conducted sometimes by Brethren pastors from nearby churches, with prayer and a great deal of singing. There were songs beloved to the conscientious objectors: "Peace I Ask of You, oh River," "Let There be Peace on Earth and Let it Begin with me," "Men of the Soil," "We Shall not be Moved," and "Like a Tree Standing by the River." In more irreverent moments we sang an anti-war song that came out of the prewar Left, "I Hate War and so does Eleanor." These Sunday evenings with the whole unit together singing were times of peace for me. I had that sense of being at one with the universe for which I still had no proper vocabulary but which lay at the base of my being. I felt a strong sense of affection for and solidarity with the other unit members, and was able to lay aside for the time being my internal dialogue about the pros and cons of being part of the unit.

The membership of the unit was always changing. A few members decided that they were no longer c.o.s and ought to be in the army; others were transferred to other units. A few got medical discharges; others arrived having recently been drafted. We had several Jehovah's Witnesses in the unit, one of whom was there at his parents' insistence. He was not really interested in either religion or pacifism; and spent his time getting drunk and figuring out what female attendant he would next seduce. Finally the administration asked Ralph to arrange for him to transfer elsewhere, an embarrassment to the c.o.s and a source of glee to the anti-conchie faction among the hospital staff.

Ralph did his best to smooth the situation over. Ralph took his responsibilities as unit leader seriously and worked at them conscientiously. Besides all the forms he had to fill out there was negotiating with top administration for the growing number of privileges the unit enjoyed, trouble-shooting for the unit members in difficulties with the selective service system, their churches, their wives, or their supervisors, and a full range of activities and outings for unit members. It was Ralph who planned the nights of singing or folk dancing, who brought us outside speakers, who helped arrange for us to attend classes in nursing and in psychiatry, who helped Allen organize a buying co-op.

As time passed, and one by one unit members lost their initial enthusiasm for making something of the experience and became apathetic, slightly withdrawn, or mildly depressed—the only way most of us could cope with our unreal environment—Ralph's efforts to keep us enthusiastic, to build a sense of the unit, to make us believe that our ordeal was somehow counting for something, became more pronounced. He was in a very real sense the life of the unit, threading our very separate and disparate selves together. Matthew told us once, candidly, that he felt most conscientious objectors had paid a price internally for their position, repressing much healthy aggression along with some not so healthy hostilities and anger. Ralph, however, he said seemed to be an exception. For a young man brought up in a strict and religious setting he seemed to be free, and to have available to him all the energies of his being.

The one thing that occasionally puzzled us about Ralph was the question of a girlfriend. He spoke of having one back home, but he never seemed to visit her, nor did she come to visit him. We were curious about her, but whenever we asked questions, he changed the subject and we felt it could not be a very serious affair. On the other hand, he was much adored by the women of the unit. We had to conclude that this side of his nature, too, he had under control. Later, when rumors began to circulate that Ralph was in love with one of the c.o. wives we laughed them off; all the wives were in love with Ralph and he was apparently quite impartial. We did not contemplate the possibility that such a thing could really be, perhaps because we did not dare.

Ours was an overheated atmosphere in regard to sex. Most of us were young and some newly married, at a time of life when sex was an all-consuming subject anyway. In addition, we heard about sex all day long from our patients who shouted words I for one had never heard before, and sometimes acted out their frustrations in full view. In the horrors of daily life on the wards some patients turned to open masturbation. Others occasionally found solace in another patient; homosexual relationships blossomed as they do in prison.

For the unmarried attendants, the sight of the married ones with arms around one another must have doubled their frustration. I once knocked rather hastily before walking into the room of a married c.o. couple only to discover the wife in the arms of another man, also a c.o., whose proper wife was six hundred miles away. A bit of a prig in those days, I was shocked and upset by the encounter. If c.o.s were claiming to live by a higher moral standard than others, demonstrating a way of life which, if lived by all, would take away the occasion for all war, as the Friends said, then ought they not to impose a discipline upon themselves relative to sexuality, I reasoned. Allen was more tolerant than I of such pecadillos. One could aim for a higher morality, he argued, just as one could aim for a nonviolent approach at all times, but one must not expect 100% compliance.

Fortunately, in the case of the tableau I had surprised, nothing further came of the relationship, and the man in question soon transferred to another unit nearer his wife. But extra-martial flirtations were rampant, and gossip about them hummed all over the hospital, especially when it concerned the c.o.s.

It was a strange time, this first summer at Sykesville. D- Day in June proved a blow to the morale of many conscientious objectors. It was hard to listen to the news from Normandy without finding oneself rooting for the Allies wholeheartedly. And if one wanted them to win so badly, what was one doing in CPS? The true horrors of Buchenwald and Belsen were still unknown, but the Russian advance was uncovering a gruesome story of the fate of the Polish Jews. Hitler was even more demonic than we had believed. He had to be stopped, and our ideas of stopping him with nonviolent means began to sound very unrealistic. We still believed that waging war meant planting dragon seeds for still other wars to come, and that World War II would lead to World War III, but sometimes I privately wondered if we had come to a place in history where humankind had no choice.

Twice in the course of the summer Allen and I had been shaken to receive a letter from a friend who had chosen to give up his c.o. status. Bob was a dear friend from Antioch days; a brilliant and gentle man whose study of history had convinced him that humankind would never outlive the twenty-first century unless war was brought to an end. But Bob had relatives in Germany who had not been heard from since 1942, and a sense of obligation to his family that ran, in his view, counter to his sense of obligation to the future. "I finally decided I owe a loyalty to this generation," he wrote us to tell us of his decision to accept non-combatant service in the army. "I won't kill, but I can be a medic and free myself from some of the guilt I feel now."

In contrast to Bob's simple statement, Ken, an old boyfriend of mine, wrote a rambling, tortured, self-justifying paper, some fifty pages long, which he mimeographed and distributed to everyone he knew, explaining his decision to enlist as a soldier, with a wistful note that perhaps it wasn't too late for him to strike a blow against Hitler. We never heard from him again; and I have often wondered if he made it.

The Ahimsa group kept in contact throughout the war years through an exchange of letters, a round robin, in which each member told his news, but more importantly discussed his "position." vis-à-vis war and pacifism. As the war dragged on and its interpretation became more complicated, so did the positions that each took. Many of the Ahimsa group had refused to register, or to be inducted into either the army or CPS camp, and were now in prison. Our prison friends had a special round robin letter, in which they debated a series of philosophic points; how far should a man go in his refusal to submit to the state? In a more justly ordered society than ours, what degree of coercion would be necessary? After the war could one find a place in society, or was it necessary to begin immediately the task of building parallel structures in order to create a less violent world? How could we develop strategies for nonviolent resistance so that another war would find us with a more clear cut alternative method for opposing evil?

In marked contrast to those of our friends and relatives in CPS, the prison letters had a surprising air of hopefulness about them. Allen thought it was because these men, by taking the ultimate step of their convictions, were freed of the guilt of a compromise which he felt he had made. They were following the Kantian imperative, acting in such a way so that if everyone acted as they did, there would not only be no war, but no support for a conscripting state. I couldn't quite go along with him, though I saw that from any standpoint CPS was a compromise.

But didn't everyone have to compromise, I argued? One of the prison letters described in detail the crisis of conscience of a c.o. in prison with one of our friends. This man had decided that it was not enough to refuse to cooperate with the state in going to prison; within prison he must keep up his witness by refusing to cooperate with the prison authorities in any way. One by one he refused to obey prison regulations until he was no longer feeding himself, but was being fed with a tube through his nose, like one of our most difficult patients on the violent ward.

The tube was plastic, and one day he saw coming down into his nose a large cockroach, which had somehow found its way into the feed mixture. Would it be an act of cooperation to call for help to keep the cockroach from swimming into his gullet? Or ought he to remain passive? He finally opted for calling for help, on the somewhat lame ground that as a vegetarian he could not destroy the life of the insect by swallowing it, but he was tortured afterwards by the feeling that he had done the wrong thing. This to me was the *reductio ad absurdum* of the notion that one could carry non-cooperation to its ultimate conclusion.

Though Allen was entering his second year in CPS, he remained in fairly good spirits. One reason for this was that we were together. Another was that he kept thinking ahead to the postwar period, when we would be free of restraints and able to make a contribution to building a better world. His father had been a conscientious objector to World War I, though, married and the father of a child, he did not face the draft. As soon as the war was over, however, he left a good job teaching architecture at the University of Pennsylvania to go overseas to help feed starving German children, as his contribution toward building a peaceful world. Allen also planned to go abroad as soon as the war was over, perhaps with the American Friends Service Committee, to play a role in postwar reconstruction.

Talk of how to rebuild the world after the war was not limited to pacifists but was in fact an engrossing subject for everyone we knew during the war years. There was still a hopefulness about in those days, a belief that humankind could do anything it set its hands to. Everyone we knew had his or her private scheme for rebuilding the world to be free of the tensions which had brought on two world wars in twenty years. The Gandhian, Ahimsa group were all for creating a wholly decentralized society, with emphasis on the small self- sustaining community. Others, more politically minded, put their faith in world government. Allen and I were still very interested in the cooperative movement, believing that building cooperatives all over the world would make it possible to counter the growing concentration of power in the state and the vast international corporations.

Our friend, Andy, shared Allen's interest in co-ops. They worked together on the co-op buying club and went together to co- op conferences. So it was to our room to talk with Allen that Andy came one night in the fall to announce that he was leaving the unit and joining the army.

"But Patton is in the Saar," said Allen, who kept up, as I didn't, with the war news. "Isn't it almost too late?" Andy, sprawled at the end of one of our cots, looked unhappy. "I'm afraid it may be, but I've got to do it," he said. "It's as necessary to me as it once was to be a c.o."

Allen looked at him quizzically. "I didn't know that you were feeling this way. You haven't said much."

"It started a long time ago," Andy said. "I realize this now, but I just wasn't willing to face it until recently. Then all of a sudden I knew I had to do something. It wasn't altogether rational."

"And yet it's reason we have to cling to now, just when its the hardest," Allen said.

"I don't know whether I think that is true anymore," Andy said. "Anyhow, mine was never a particularly well-reasoned position. I had faith, Allen, and I lost it here, and without faith, a strong religious faith, I just don't see that the c.o. stand makes much sense."

"Hershey would agree with you," Allen said drily. I knew he was thinking of our friends in prison to whom c.o. status had been denied because their draft boards had judged their reasons for claiming c.o. status to be too philosophical. I knew, too, that he still regretted the ease with which his Quaker background had won him his status. He continued to believe that the basis of his own position to be more philosophic than religious in the strict sense of the word.

"It's possible for some guys to have a deeply held stand against war without religious faith, I guess, but not for me," Andy said. "It doesn't make any sense to me. I look around the hospital and all I see is cruelty and dishonesty and violence. How can you talk about building a world without war when the human material we have to work with is so faulty."

"Nobody's talking about the coming of the kingdom, at least for a while," Allen said. "We're talking about finding more mature and rational ways for humankind to solve problems. War is a stone-age method and it won't work anymore. Everyone knows that the vengefulness of the Allies at Versailles created the paranoia among the German people on which Hitler fed. It will all happen over again. We know that."

"We'll have to come some day to some sort of world govern-ment," Andy said. "But I've been thinking a lot, and I think it will have to be based on law backed up by force. We can't just pretend the evil isn't there. It's got to be faced and dealt with."

"Gandhi dealt with evil without resorting to violence," Allen pointed out.

"Gandhi was up against a nation of gentlemen," Andy said. "And he was up against them literally, face to face. What sort of nonviolent persuasion are you going to exercise on the bomber pilot 4,000 feet above your head?"

"But you're trying to project the pacifist solution into a non pacifist world," Allen argued. "What we are saying is that if every-one acted as we do there would be no bomber pilot overhead."

"But how are you going to convert the world to this way of thinking when we haven't even been able to win over anyone in this hospital?" Andy asked "How can we, how can you expect to convert anyone in fact when none of us can practice it ourselves. You begin to believe in someone here and then, poof! It's a sure sign you are going to find out something about him that rocks your whole faith in mankind."

"Are you talking about someone in particular?" Allen asked.

"O no, just in general," Andy said. But I had a sudden strong intuition that someone he trusted had let him down.

"A couple of things which one of my professors in college said stick with me," Allen said. I could see that he was wound up in the argument and unaware of the nuances in what Andy was trying to tell us. "He quoted Eric Fromm as saying that the luxury of pure belief was behind us. We would have to get along from now on acting with conviction even if we were only 51% sure. And the other thing--and it's closely related--was that we would have to learn to accept our historic role and maybe not struggle to make it universal. Maybe we'll never convert everyone, but if we stick with our principles we'll be a force for change, for the development of world government. We'll balance out the forces of militarism on the right. We'll help the moderate center to grow strong. That's not the stuff the old crusaders depended on, but it's the best we can hope for."

Andy shook his head. He admired Allen, I knew, and was impressed with his argument. Still, the whole conversation seemed to have little to do with his decision. "Maybe some people can manage on 51% he said. "I can't. I have to be sure. I have to have a faith, and now I've lost it. There really isn't anything more to it than that."

Allen looked perplexed for a moment, then his face cleared and lit with a smile. "I guess I'm no help trying to talk you out of it," he said. "I guess all I can do is wish you luck and say that we'll miss you, Andy."

Andy got up from the bed and rather awkwardly offered his hand to Allen. They shook warmly, Andy thanked us for our patience, and turned toward the door. I noticed how his shoulders drooped. I realized how he must be dreading the army, and hated partings like this.

"Seems pretty mixed up to me," Allen commented after Andy had left.

"I don't know, Allen, I think we're all pretty mixed up," I said. "The more I think about it the more I agree with Andy, that you have to go on what you feel more than what you think."

"That's not very logical, Marge. You've always been so logical," Allen said.

"I know," I said miserably, "but I'm beginning to think there is more to it than logic."

"Like what?"

"Like intuition, like deep genuine feelings, like what people mean when they talk about the spirit."

"And where do these feelings lead you now?"

"I don't know, Allen," I said, as miserable as Andy. "They lead me in Andy's direction, I guess. Like I can't quite trust all our theories any more until I can come to trust myself."

Someone else came into the room just then, and the conversation ended. Perhaps it was just as well, for such conversations turned too often these days into quarrels. Whenever I was upset about the war I felt the need to attack what seemed to me like Allen's complacency. The result was that we were both miserable.

But though we never discussed Andy's departure again, it continued to trouble me. I began to wonder if each of us was forever trapped into a hall of mirrors, seeing about himself or herself nothing but the reflections of our self image. Some people like Ralph and perhaps Allen saw only the best in others because that was their image of themselves. Andy and I saw the worst. There must be a thousand grades of distortions and confusions in between. How then could we expect to build a new world when we could not agree on the nature of the basic building block, the human personality?

A state mental hospital is not the best setting in which to convince oneself that people are basically good. Most of the patients

were too wrapped up in their own problems to concern themselves at all about their fellow patients, although every now and
then we saw a heartwarming example of such concern. The relatives whom I interviewed often seemed to me more concerned
about themselves than about the patients. Doctors, nurses, social
workers all to varying extents inured themselves against feeling
much sympathy for either patients or relatives. This was under-
standable; if you allowed yourself to experience the full pain these
people were going through, you yourself would be a basket case by
the end of the day. But it seemed to me that most went to the
other extreme and became brittle and unfeeling, keeping the tide
of human misery in which we lived at a great distance through a
sort of gallows humor, and a distain for people who allowed themselves to become out of control "crazies."

And of course there were the attendants, a few kindly but the
majority angry at being in their jobs, and taking the anger out on
their charges. For many the range seemed to be from indifference
to outright cruelty , from Mrs. Porter whose only concern was
keeping her ward clean and her floors gleaming to Mrs. Jones, the
bully of South II-A. I had learned to recognize that fear often lay
behind the treatment some attendants visited on their patients,
but this fact did not lessen the evil, any more than the German
peoples resentment of the Treaty of Versailles justified their treatment of the Jews.

Worst of all, I had learned to recognize that I was capable of
being motivated by fear into acting in ways I regretted. I still had
a long way to go before I achieved self knowledge, but I had some
inklings that I could not base faith in the goodness of human
nature on myself. I was still often miserably unsure of myself,
needing approval, and blind sometimes to what I did to other
people who got in the way when I was concentrating on relieving
that need.

Allen would have said I was too critical of myself as well as of
others; and that by concentrating on their worst traits I blinded
myself to their best qualities. People were a mixture of both good
and evil, he believed. One didn't have to delude oneself that there

was no evil, but only concentrate on bringing out the good. If there were occasional slips, well that was part of the human condition. But until we had a society that was more just and peaceful it was hard to ascertain what basic human nature was really like.

Allen was basically an optimist about people. He liked them, and forgave them their faults. He did not articulate it, but he operated on the fundamental Quaker assumption that there is that of God in everyone. Somehow, despite the agnosticism of my mother, I had picked up some of the Calvinism of my Scotch Presbyterian ancestors, with its pessimism about human nature. For me, humans, including myself, were inclined to sin, and needed the restraint of a strict moral code in order to behave properly. To me the cup of human nature was half empty, to him, half full. I was a perfectionist; he was willing to accept people as they were, while constantly hoping for the best. I could sometimes see this, but I remained uneasy that pacifism demanded a striving for a level of human perfection which seemed unreachable to me. I thought about Andy often in the weeks that followed, and I often felt troubled by his decision to leave.

Chapter VII

$\mathcal{T}$HERE WERE TIMES when it had seemed as though that summer at Sykesville would last forever. Days of sticky, humid summer heat followed upon one another through August and September. The Hubner building baked in the hot summer sun and it became breathless on the wards, the heat exaggerating the smells which were never quite drowned out by Klomine. Nor did it cool down at night, and our little room in the Epileptic Colony held the heat of the day and became an oven. We had asked our parents to send a fan, and went to sleep each night to its whirr, and the slight breeze it created as it passed over us on the bed in its endless cycle.

Even at Sykesville, however, fall came eventually. Perhaps because we had waited so long and impatiently for it, it seemed a particularly beautiful fall, with crisp cool mornings, brilliant days, bright sunsets. There were few trees on the Sykesville grounds, but beyond the rolling Maryland hills were tree covered, and we watched as the first few patches of scarlet appeared, as the elms added their clear yellow, and the oaks joined in with oranges and browns. Allen and I took a twenty-five mile bike ride to see an Antioch friend who had just been released from prison and was living with his wife in the home of a federal prison official, near Washington. The trip through the sea of fall color was so enchanting I was able to forgive and forget how sore the men's saddle made me. We had a wonderful reunion with our friends, and best of all, they were able to borrow a car and drive us back.

Not far from the hospital there was an abandoned apple orchard on a hill where we often went on our day off to search for drops, which we would make into applesauce on our illegal hot plates, and to look over the countryside around us. I remember one Saturday going there with the Durdens and Jim. The hay had been mowed, and after gathering our fill of slightly wormy apples, we lay in the stubble near the trees, munching apples and looking up into the cloudless sky. It was so perfect, that I was suddenly at peace. The moment began to expand, became eternal. I felt an ineffable sweetness, yet a sadness, and recognized the sort of opening I had had before. There was something beyond myself that I sometimes touched, as a swimmer touches bottom, and when I did, I felt it was the only reality. I finally came back to my friends as though I had been on a long journey. Later I wrote a poem about it, but the words did not capture that moment of complete joy.

The fall was a time of new beginnings. We moved from our cramped quarters in the Epileptic Colony to a larger and more pleasant room in the new Attendants' Building. The Durdens moved next door, and several other C.O. couples, down the hall. We were at last rid of our hostile neighbors, and their embarrassing habit of pounding on our wall at night, and we had better bathroom facilities and a laundry and bowling alley in our basement. We decorated our new room with care, buying coarse colored burlap for drapes and spreads, tacking up more Van Gogh reprints, and invited unit members to come and see us.

Matthew decided to offer a ten-week course on the dynamics of interpersonal relationships that fall, and we both signed up, glad to have reading assignments and papers to write again. Matthew based his teaching on the work of Harry Stack Sullivan, but he ranged broadly, and we read widely in the field. Our acquaintance with the work of Karen Horney and Eric Fromm goes back to this period. Some of the students went with Matthew to an occasional lecture in Washington, but we never could afford this. However, the course was probably responsible for our life-long interest in psychology.

After Andy left to join the army, Allen became the principal mover that fall in the small attendants' buying club. By purchasing hand soap, tooth paste, laundry soap, writing paper, and similar supplies, the club was able to achieve some real savings; particularly needed by the single men who were trying to survive on eleven dollars a month. The buying club had regular meetings, and Allen felt that the participants learned something at least about economic democracy. I was proud of him and liked to see him preside at the meetings. Sometimes I felt he wasn't getting the recognition he deserved from the rest of the c.o.s. He was too different and perhaps in some ways too distant from the preponderance of fairly unsophisticated men, mostly from farm backgrounds, who peopled our unit. But he was interested in them all and fond of a few, and wifelike I wanted them to recognize his worth.

The unit was dispirited that fall. The majority of conscientious objectors had been at Sykesville since early in 1942, and were therefore approaching a third anniversary at the hospital. The allies were having setbacks; who knew when and if this war would ever end? And would the government release all c.o.s when it was over, or keep them as an additional form of punishment? As Allen pointed out in a letter to his parents, most c.o.s seemed to become bitter and withdrawn after their first year of duty. The inherent frustration of being a pacifist in wartime, and of being conscripted to perform a service of questionable value, took its toll.

Morale was a major problem throughout CPS. In the hospital units we had the company and stimulation of at least some doctors and social workers and a few of the attendants; and the sense that our work had validity. In the isolated CPS camps devoted to forestry and the like the men had only each other and endless talk to batter down morale, and some task such as planting seedlings, which seemed far removed from the priorities of the day.

As the war dragged on, and c.o.s became ever more unpopular with the general public, the Selective Service administration came up with more and more petty rules to prevent the objectors from intermingling with, or annoying that public. There were rules curtailing leaves and travel and the like and the camp director and his assistant, appointed by the peace church in question, had the unenviable job of enforcing these rules on frustrated, unhappy men.

This highlighted a question that began to bother many conscientious objectors; were not the peace churches complicit in the conscription system by playing this role? Particularly in the Quaker camps, where the men were of a more questioning frame of mind than elsewhere, this question was hotly debated, and much anger was projected at the American Friends Service Committee for helping to create the system, and serving as its accomplice. We received more letters from more old friends outlining their dissatisfaction with the system and in some cases their decision to walk out of CPS camp as a result. This point of view became so widespread that the peace churches never attempted such an experiment again. Instead, during the Korean and Vietnamese wars, a vastly larger number of c.o.s confronted their draft boards directly and were placed in individual assignments.

Members of our hospital unit, in touch with friends in the more isolated CPS camps, heard about the debate and it further lowered morale. Had the Brethren Church made a great mistake in placing us here, and in agreeing to the $11.00 a month pay? Ought Ralph to be enforcing the rules governing leaves?

In the late fall, an ugly episode occurred to further depress us. As the work force steadily fell, the administration was forced to hire more and more questionable employees, men who were themselves dried out alcoholics or drifters in need of earning a few bucks. One such man, hired as a night attendant at the Hubner building, turned out to be a sadist; patients were beaten and choked with a rubber hose when they offended him. When found out, he attempted to shift the blame to one of the c.o.s assigned to night duty. The allegations of brutality were investigated and the c.o. eventually exonerated, but not before rumors had spread throughout the hospital that one of the conchies had beaten up a patient. We experienced, as a result, a new flare up of anti-c.o. feeling. The war was dragging on; the wives of servicemen were suffering frustration and despair; the "yellow bellies" were a near and easy target. There was an outbreak of unpleasantness in the attendants' dining room, remarks were made loudly as we passed some of the more intransigent in the halls, tensions mounted.

It was about this time that Allen and I had the first serious quarrel of our young married life. We had gone with Alice and Sam to spend an evening with Matthew and Liz. They showed us slides of a recent trip they had made and served us a milk punch, called "tiger's milk" they had recently discovered. Although it tasted mild, it was lethal in its effect, especially on people like ourselves who were unused to strong liquor. After a cup full or so I began to feel dizzy and begged off, but Allen kept drinking it enthusiastically, and I thought he was beginning to sound tipsy.

"I'm afraid we'd better leave," I announced. "Allen has to be on the ward by six a.m."

"Oh, why so soon?" Allen said. "Let's make a night of it."

He was slurring his speech slightly, and the others were amused.

"At least have one for the road," Alice suggested mischievously.

"O, Allen, I think we've had enough," I said. It was a challenge of wifely authority, and Allen had had enough of authority, wifely or other.

He looked at me, looked at Alice, winked, and downed a large glassful of tiger's milk.

A feeling of desolation swept over me. I felt both humiliated and deserted. Was it for this I had left my exciting life in New York and had subjected myself to the rigors of Sykesville? We managed to make our goodbyes civil, but stepping out into the frosty night our tempers flared. Allen was angry that I had tried to control him so blatantly in public, I that he had deliberated cho-sen Alice's advice over mine. I felt she had done it in the spirit of a contest of power, and he had let her win. I also felt myself totally alone. We shouted at each other, raking up old wounds, and I ran away from him, and walked by myself through the grounds in the cold moonlight until I was too exhausted to walk further, and knew there was no place to go but back to our stuffy room. Here I found Allen sound asleep, little disturbed by our frightening quarrel.

We made it up of course the next day, and for many weeks we seemed to be reknit. But a basic problem in our marriage, my need for the reassurance of exclusive loyalty; Allen's for freedom from the bonds of intimacy, had been exposed. Tiger's milk became a family watchword for certain kinds of trouble, and the aftermath of the quarrel lingered as we continued to struggle with the meaning of Sykesville in our lives.

With the coming of shorter days and colder weather, the patients who were depressed and withdrawn seemed more so. On South II-A a slender little woman was found hanging by her belt by the first light of dawn. Another patient, a man who had been at the hospital for a long time, and who was in charge of keeping the attendants' dining room clean, was given shock treatments and seemed to be improving. He talked a little at meal times for the first time in months, telling me once a bit about his daughter. But when we came over for breakfast a few days later we learned that he had been found early that morning in the broom closet with his wrists slashed, and blood everywhere. The doctors explained that the shock treatments had begun to cure his deep depression, and that the patient recovered enough to find his will to end his own life. We had all liked Jim, and the explanation did nothing for our sense of outrage.

It was at this time, too, that two events occurred almost simultaneously to augment our gloom. A very sick and withdrawn, but very pretty young pregnant woman had been admitted in the spring and had given birth to a baby in the course of the summer. The doctors had tried to persuade the husband to sign papers for her sterilization, since she already had three children, but he was adamant. Shortly, against all medical advice, he checked his wife out of the hospital for a day, and then brought her back to us. Several months later we discovered she was pregnant once more. A day or two after this discovery we had another admission, a twenty-one year old girl who had been born at this hospital, of a schizophrenic mother and now returned, withdrawn, hostile and hallucinating. Was the hospital just a revolving door through which generations of patients came and went? It seemed that fall as though all the patients triumphantly discharged during the spring or summer were returning, sicker than ever. It was hard to believe that what we were doing had much worth after all.

In my admissions interviews I was supposed to ask about the patient's sex life. I thought the question was objectionable, and I was amazed at how fully and frankly it was usually answered. I learned much that way. One thing that surprised me was that the Catholic families used artificial birth control methods as a matter of course, and seemed unaware, even, that the church had any position on the matter. When the husband refused sterilization for his very ill wife, it was not on religious grounds, but apparently because he perceived it as an invasion of his privacy.

I continued to learn more about people and about myself as I worked in the admissions office. Each admission was a fresh glimpse into some form or other of human tragedy, depressingly the same, and yet each different enough to intrigue me in trying to discover, through my interviews, the story behind the story. As I became more experienced I learned to ask the right questions so that the response was a torrent of information; once I started the interview I often did not need to do any prodding in order to get more than enough for the hospital's purposes. The spilling out seemed to make the relatives feel much better. After such a session they were often more amenable to thinking about the patient's return to the community.

I began finally to revise my view of the relatives, whom I had originally felt were self-centered, caring more about their own esteem than that of the patient. I felt more empathetic with their own crisis of emotions at the juncture of admission, and to understand that they had a private agenda they had to get off their chests in order to get on with the agenda of the hospital. This increased sympathy of course communicated itself to the relatives, and I got even more interesting and detailed case histories as a result.

Admissions always came in spurts. When they were slow I spent time chatting with Dr. Wiseman, whose office was next to mine, mainly answering or parrying his probing questions about me and my life. As he and the other doctors got to know me better, they began to find ways to use my time. They taught me to give some simple psychological tests, and even to conduct non-directive counseling sessions with recovering patients. This was not difficult, all I had to do was learn to listen.

Matilda had developed an in-hospital job placement program in which I also sometimes participated. The idea was to find work in the farm buildings or the laundry elsewhere for patients who were well enough to participate. The theory was that this prepared them for work outside the hospital when they recovered further. The fact was that they contributed to the smooth and inexpensive running of the hospital, since they were not paid for their work. I had interviews with several of them, supposedly preparing them for the job situation, and encouraging them to think of a job as a step toward leaving the hospital. This did not always reassure the patient. One young epileptic had a spectacular series of seizures after my visit, according to his doctor. But at least it got me occasionally out of the office and onto the grounds.

Matilda expressed herself as being delighted with my progress, and suggested that I write a paper on my job, to be entitled "The Locus and Function of the Psychiatric Social Worker in the Admissions Office." In our weekly supervisory sessions she was teaching me a great deal of Otto Rank's theory of social work, emphasizing the use of the time of the interview as a dynamic in a growth process that was supposed to be taking place, and the importance of the interviewer understanding her exact role, or locus, in the equation. Writing the paper, she explained, would be an additional way of gaining education in social work theory, equivalent to that I would receive if I decided to enroll in a school of social work, especially, of course, Pennsylvania School of Social Work. Perhaps I should have been warned by the brightness of her smile that her motives were mixed, but I was flattered and agreed readily enough to try my hand.

As month followed month, I began to build up a file of case histories which I regarded as my best work, or felt might be helpful to illustrate some point. After my interview with Matilda I went over these, looking for case history material with which to illustrate such a paper. We had been studying symbolism in our evening courses with Matthew, discovering how patients unconsciously searched for and found symbols to express their deepest conflicts. I recently had conducted an interview with the sister of a patient, and had found the story rife with symbolism. I drew the history out now and read it through again.

An elderly woman had come to the hospital one day bringing her slightly older brother who was consumed with a dreadful anxiety. A dozen times a day, she told me, and more than that often at night, he had gone down to the cellar of their little house to check the pipes and make sure that none would burst. He called the plumber repeatedly, but none of the plumber's adjustments and none of his reassurances would help. Recently the brother had become even more obsessed with his fear and would allow no one, not even the plumber, to touch the lip of the faucets.

The anxiety appeared to be a product of advancing age. There had been no previous episodes. "We worked hard and had only a little money," the sister told me, "but we were happy and we loved each other dearly. Only. . . ." Only during the last unhappy months the brother's love had begun to express itself in strange ways. He would seize his sister and kiss her hard on the mouth in a way that confused and frightened her. And he was jealous if she spoke even to the milkman. And the terrible worry about the bursting pipes escalated.

The pipes of course were seen by the doctors to represent the patient's long-repressed libidinal feelings for his sister bursting out of control. "Wow, it's too good to be true," Dr. Wiseman said when he saw the history and he asked for a copy for a course he was teaching in the city. The other doctors liked it, too, and it was used as a classic case to illustrate the origins of anxiety when the prohibitions of a lifetime began to crumble in the face of advancing age. I had a worried feeling that they were making it too simple, and that it certainly did not guide us in ways to help the poor bewildered brother and sister. Still, it would certainly look good in my paper.

I was still looking for a suitable case the day I talked with Arabella's aunt. Arabella was a young woman of about thirty brought to us from a private mental hospital. A thick file came with her chronicling other hospitalizations and medical records, but I searched in vain for any social history, or any record of members of her family involving themselves in her care. My original letters to her parents, who lived in a different state, were ignored, but I was persistent, and finally made contact with an aunt who lived in Baltimore, and had evidently taken more interest in Arabella than anyone else.

The doctors were puzzled by Arabella, who seemed withdrawn but didn't quite fit any pattern of schizophrenia. They also badly wanted permission to administer shock therapy, as usual. They were therefore pleased when I discovered the aunt, and eager that I learn all I could from her.

The aunt turned out to be a rather dumpy little woman, with a wide but vague smile, a determination to look at the bright side of everything, and practically no information to give us. She was an artist, she told me, and kept a small arts and crafts shop. She was also a Christian Scientist and could not possibly sign for shock treatments. She was fond of Arabella, and angry that her parents had simply discarded her from their lives, but she didn't know if she could be of much help.

I had the distinct impression that the little woman knew more than she was admitting. How could one be as close to a sick relative as she had been to Arabella, according to her own account, and not have given some thought to her childhood? I tried all the various tricks I had learned to prime the pump of revelation; asking questions that appeared unrelated but might bring a stream of memory. "What do you most often think of her doing when you saw her as a child?" I told stories that might be analogous, and I tried to let the aunt lead the conversation, to see if she would bring it around to what was on her mind. Nothing worked. The aunt seemed eager to please but devoid of helpful insights.

Finally, in desperation, I decided to try a method I had once or twice found effective, psychological shock.

"I don't feel we are getting very far, Mrs. Stroble," I said severely. "After all, we already know a great deal about Arabella, which we are not discussing here. We know for instance that at age twenty she had an illegimate baby which was put up for adoption."

The little woman sat up straight in her chair across from me, and her eyes popped with surprise. I realized in sudden horror that I had revealed a family secret long kept from her, and kept, perhaps, for good reason. Moreover it was immediately apparent to me that she was going to use her new knowledge. "That they would block her natural urge toward motherhood!" she exclaimed, her eyes flashing angrily. "O, I cannot wait to confront them with this. Thank you, Mrs. Bacon, I believe you have cleared up the mystery."

"But that was more than ten years ago, and surely it does no good to bring it up now," I said, wondering if there was any way I could undo the mischief I had done. But no, Mrs. Stroble was as happy as a cat with a wounded mouse. She bid me good day almost immediately, and trotted off without once asking about Arabella. She not only had not given me any information, or signed for shock treatment, but had shown no signs of interest in helping her niece readjust after the hospital, no interest at all, period. I had evidently blundered into a family feud.

I told Allen about it that night, feeling wretched. "I've meddled in a private affair and I've probably caused trouble that will last a lifetime, and to what end?" I accused myself. "So that I could get some more details for my case history."

"It was a natural thing to do," Allen soothed. "You didn't realize it was a secret. In most families things like that are known."

But I was not to be consoled so easily. "If there was something she needed to tell me I should have helped her to get it out naturally," I worried, "That was a violent way to attack her. Even if it had worked it was still a way of using violence. The truth is I'm afraid I don't really care all that much what means I use so long as I get the results I want. I'm just as bad as Dr. Wiseman and his shock machine."

For the balance of the week I continued to feel uncomfortable about the session and I began to wonder if there were something I could do to remedy my mistake. Talk again with the aunt? Write the family once more, urging them to come in so that I could confess in person about the interview? Neither course of action seemed appropriate, and I decided to consult Matilda at our next supervisory conference. Matilda, however, was no help to my guilty conscience. That was what I was suffering from, she told me, guilt: I was wallowing in it rather than trying to look at the circumstances realistically. After all, I had been trying to get information to help the doctors to help the patient. If I had erred in revealing something from a confidential chart it was a normal error which I would only exaggerate and make worse by any further action. She advised me to dismiss the matter from my mind. If I couldn't do so then I was suffering from generalized guilt, attaching a free floating anxiety to a trifling incident.

"Perhaps I am," I told her dryly. I was aware of a slight shift in our relationship and a tightening of tension between us. Until now she had been the queen, bestowing generous amounts of encouragement and praise on my progress reports, explaining to me in flattering terms her appraisal of my "growth" and "perceptions." I, on my part, like the rest of the social workers, had been ready to lap it up, to admire her, and to be putty in her hands. Now suddenly a small knot of resistance was hardening in me. My feelings of guilt were my own, and appropriate; I had done a foolish and hurtful thing. I would not have my conscience wallpapered over and smoothed away.

Matilda saw my resistance as stubbornness. "But you've always been so open, so fluid, " she pouted, "I don't understand this rigidity."

"Maybe I ought to talk to Matthew about it," I suggested.

"Not Matthew!" Matilda said hurriedly, and I saw that she had something at stake. Rather than prolong an interview which was destined to get me nowhere I decided to shift the subject and talk about my paper. Normally Matilda could not be diverted, but that paper was her pride and joy, and telling her about my progress with it made her so happy she forgot about my resistance.

But I was not through with the incident. Though I soon concluded that there was nothing indeed to do but put it behind me, it continued to fester in my conscience like a tiny thorn, making me progressively less delighted with my job in the admissions office. If I could indeed help husbands or wives, mothers or fathers, sweethearts or sisters, brothers or friends, to feel a bit more comfortable about the hospitalization of their loved one that was a goal worth realizing, I thought. But to use their grief, their guilt, their abstraction to get from them something that the hospital wanted—a case history permission to use shock therapy, blanket permission for experimental treatments—that was manipulative. I had very little faith in the hospital's treatment procedures, and I had evidence clearly before me that my splendid case histories made not one whit of difference in the way we treated patients— nine times out of ten it was shock therapy anyway. No, the purpose of the histories was to please myself and possibly the doctors, and certainly Matilda, to delude ourselves that we were basing our approach to the patient on an understanding of her problems, never actually to help the patient herself.

Once formed, the cancer of doubt spread. I began to see the whole community of Sykesville as based on exploiting the patients. Where would the jobs be for the refugee doctors, for the local villagers who worked on the wards, for the conscientious objectors who wanted to do useful work in wartime, if it weren't for the patients? How could the hospital floors be kept shining? the farm worked, the cows milked, the garbage dumped, the apartments cleaned, the food cooked, without them? It was suddenly possible to see the whole world of the hospital as a kingdom served by patients whom we turned into slaves to the system by our own definitions of them. And like conquering colonial powers everywhere, we hid our guilt from ourselves by assuring ourselves that we were doing everything possible for the exploited.

Was that, I wondered, why guilt was the one unacceptable emotion here? For indeed if you began to look around there were crude demands for honest, human guilt on every side. Patients were incorrectly strapped for their shock treatments and got broken legs and backs as a result. One patient was kept too long at too high a temperature in hydrotherapy and died shortly after treatment from a heart attack. Suicidal patients were not watched carefully enough and managed to do away with themselves, though in the admissions office we often explained soothingly that such a thing could not happen here, that the patient was being protected from himself.

As if to reinforce these worries of mine, the medical staff embarked that winter on a new experiment in the treatment of patients: prefrontal lobotomy. In this relatively simple but frightening operation, holes were drilled in either side of the patient's skull, and a very fine knife inserted and used to disconnect portions of the forebrain. As explained to us by Dr. Wiseman, no one understood exactly what happened but it appeared to relieve patients who were suffering from an overload of guilt and anxiety. After a successful lobotomy a patient might become cheerful and carefree, some sufficiently so to return to normal life. Sometimes they were rather vegetable-like in their new state, but better, Dr. Wiseman thought, a happy vegetable than a disturbed patient.

We c.o.s read and heard more about lobotomies, and what we learned was not reassuring. Sometimes the little knife slipped, and then the patient might be deprived of his power of speech or association. Or, even when the lobes had been severed, there appeared to be a tendency for the patient to revert quickly to his former state. In fact, the doctors knew as little about the procedure's long-term effect as they knew about shock.

This, however, did not deter our medical group at Sykesville. Matthew was as usual opposed, believing lobotomy to be a form of treatment that had all the earmarks of barbarism, and a procedure about which we knew very little if at all about its permanent effect. The rest, however, were terribly excited. Dr. Wiseman went to Washington to take some special training in the surgical procedure, and upon his return the doctors began to experiment, using as their guinea pigs patients from the Men's Group or Women's Group whose condition had not changed for thirty years. Of course the family had to be hunted up, and permission obtained, but the medical staff did not turn this job over to me, or any of the other social workers, who shared my skepticism. The operations were performed it seemed with a certain amount of secrecy, and we heard little about them.

I talked with Allen from time to time about my disturbing new view of the hospital. Allen agreed with me, but did not share quite the passion. He did not, I saw, have as much reason for feeling complicit as I. Patients might be exploited in the admissions office for the sake of case histories and shock therapy permission, or in the staff meeting for the sake of diagnoses, or on most of the wards for the sake of polished floors. In South I-A they were treated as decently as possible. Allen and Sam and Adam, who had taken Andy's place on the ward, were frustrated by the war, by conscription, by the endless waiting until the job of building a new world could begin, but they could not help having some sense of satisfaction for the kind of care they extended their patients. South I-A continued to be the quietest ward in the Huboer Group, mystifying all the doctors but Matthew.

One day, during this period of turmoil in myself, while waiting for an appointment with a family member who was late in showing up, I decided to talk about my feelings with Ralph. I came into his office rather suddenly and ran into Sally, Adam's wife, talking earnestly to Ralph. I had the impression that she was discussing some confidential problem and started to excuse myself and turn away, but she flashed her brilliant smile and urged me to stay, she was just going. Ralph followed her with his eyes to the door, then turned to me.

"I hear they did another lobotomy last night," I ventured.

"Yes, I heard that," Ralph said.

"Every time that happens I suddenly feel as though we weren't part of a hospital at all; more like helping to shore up the Spanish Inquisition," I said.

Ralph smiled. Just like Marge, I could see him thinking, always exaggerating. "It does seem pretty bad," he admitted, "but after all, I understand the ones they are working on don't have much of a chance, anyway."

"Maybe everyone has the right to be miserable in her own way," I suggested.

Ralph reached across the desk for a tabloid. "Have you seen *The Attendant?*" he asked. "Some guys in the Friends unit at Byberry have started it up. They say CPS will be a failure unless the c.o.s start some mental hospital reform. Sounds up your alley, Marge. Maybe you could write about lobotomies for them." I took a copy of the newspaper and glanced over it. Articles on overcrowding, articles on the pros and cons of shock therapy; an article on a nondirective approach to patients. It did indeed look interesting to me. It was exactly like Ralph to know what to recommend, and I told him so.

His smile, I thought, was a little rueful. "I guess we all have some knacks, but we all have our weaknesses, too," he said.

"All except you," I said laughing.

"Don't say that," he asked seriously. "Please don't say that."

I was puzzled by his expression, and might have pushed the conversation further, but just then a call came from the front office that Mrs. Bacon was needed; her 3 p.m. appointment had at last arrived. I thanked Ralph for *The Attendant*, started, hesitated at the door, then decided against saying anything and hurried to my office.

I never did write for *The Attendant*. Things happened shortly after this interview which drove the project from my mind. But I was proud years later to learn that from this Byberry Unit had grown a whole new organization devoted to improving public understanding of mental health and to reforming the state hospitals. The development of community-based mental health treatment and the effort to move patients out of the warehousing hospitals and into the community, called deinstitutionalization, was hastened by this development. It took young people, coming into the hospitals in large numbers, to begin to see that the institution itself could be a system that created dependency rather than health. This insight swam against the perceived wisdom of the day; psychiatrists and social workers were united at the time in believing the hospital environment itself was therapeutic, just as Matilda kept saying.

Sykesville was regarded, and certainly regarded itself, as a modern, progressive institution.

But the conscientious objectors were not easily swayed. They expressed themselves, and so did other brave souls. Over the years the movement to move patients out of the giant hospitals gathered strength. When the history of recent mental health progress is reviewed, the role of the conscientious objectors during World War II is often mentioned.

People have sometimes asked me, why, if I saw that getting permission for shock therapy was wrong, did I continue to do so? And why didn't I speak out against lobotomy? I can only look back and think that I was too unsure of my own responses, too eager to please, to act on my deepest insights. I hated being a marginal person; to have been a whistle blower I would have become even more marginal. But I am glad I at least raised questions at the time.

Chapter VIII

*T*HE IDEA OF A RETREAT BEGAN AS A JOKE. The Durdens and we were playing poker one night in the Attendants' Quarters when Ralph dropped by for a visit. He seemed more restless that winter than he had before, and at times more withdrawn, while at other times he craved company. He was reading constantly and sought out either Allen or Sam to talk about books. On this occasion he came to return Gandhi's autobiography and see if Sam had anything else to recommend.

"Nothing comes to mind unless you want to try Nietzsche," Sam drawled. Sam was in one of his anti-intellectual moods. Aside from playing poker he wanted to talk only about what kind of a car he would buy when the war ended, if it ever ended, and what kind of a house he would like to build.

"We ought to start a great books discussion group," Ralph said, rather tentatively, I thought.

"Hit me again," Sam said to Allen, who was dealing.

"That's a good idea, Ralph," Allen replied. "I don't know, though, do you think there's really enough interest in the unit to make it worthwhile?"

Ralph shrugged. "Maybe not on a regular basis," he said, "but maybe we could have an occasional weekend or so. Which reminds me, I had a call today from someone at the Brethren Service Committee. It seems there is a farm house which is used during the summer for church retreats and what not that they aren't

117

using presently and thought some people from our unit might like to plan a retreat there."

"I'm all for that if we can play poker," Sam said.

"And drink beer," Allen added wickedly.

Ralph looked slightly pained, and the topic was dismissed, but a few days later we began to talk about it more seriously. Ralph had discussed the option with several other groups within the unit and they were planning to spend a weekend at the farmhouse, we learned. The idea of getting away from the hospital and out into the country for a few days began to sound enticing, and it didn't seem quite fair to go for a frivolous vacation at the expense of the good Brethren. Maybe a retreat could serve to give us time away from the hospital together with a chance to do a little thinking about our future.

In addition to ourselves and the Durdens we decided to ask Adam and Sally, Charlie and Janet, Jim, and Ralph. Adam said he wasn't sure, Sally hadn't been feeling very well but he hoped they could make it. Charlie and Janet were enthusiastic, and Charlie began to plan songs we could sing and religious poetry we could read, much as though we were a bona fide young Methodist group. Jim seemed happy to be included. Only Ralph, of all people, turned us down.

"But you were the one to suggest it!" I said to him, genuinely puzzled. "We really had you in mind when we first began to talk about it as a possibility. You know, you've always wanted to have a time when you could talk to Sam and Allen about some of the stuff you have been reading."

"I appreciate that, but you know, Marge, I am so involved in the unit that the best thing I can do is get away for a couple of days by myself," Ralph said earnestly. "I sometimes think it might be time for me to transfer to another unit, and let someone else have a turn at the directorship."

"You can't be serious," I told him. "We probably have the highest morale rate for a CPS unit East of the Rockies, and it's all due to you."

"That's not true," Ralph said sharply.

But sorry though we were to face the weekend without him, we were too far along in our plans to turn back. We had selected the last weekend in March, hoping for good weather. Spring came early in that corner of Maryland and we thought we might have a first taste of it if we were lucky. At any rate, we had to plan food for nine of us, and arrange the logistics of getting people, food, and baggage transported some twenty-five miles with one borrowed, beat up Chevrolet to make the trip. Ralph gave us the key to the place and Alice, Janet and I went over early to give it a quick cleaning, and to lay in a supply of firewood for the kitchen stove.

The farmhouse which the Brethren had offered us was ramshackle and quite old. One stepped down from the living area to the kitchen, and up to the fireplace hearth. The stairs were tiny, the windows had beautiful imperfections in the old glass, and the kitchen was abutted by a series of sheds. It would have been charming, but it needed the loving touch of devoted occupants. Empty except for small church groups like ours, it was clean enough but sterile, and smelled a bit of mice and must. Here and there were incongruous touches—abandoned blackboards, bedraggled badminton nets—which spoke of its present function.

Friday when Alice, Janet and I went over to clean, it was cloudy and quite cold, and that night it began to rain a steady, dispirited cold rain which continued off and on throughout the weekend. The house was unheated except for a couple of electric heaters you could plug into wall sockets, the kitchen stove and the fireplace. Janet, who had been a farm girl, taught us how to lay a fire in the stove, and how to bank it for overnight use. There was also a smelly kerosene stove on which we did our cooking. We wore heavy sweaters and slacks, played ping pong to keep warm, and managed to survive, but we were constantly chilly.

Despite these discomforts, however, it was good to be away from the hospital and together, and Saturday passed in a happy fashion, with much laughter. Sally, I noticed, seemed a little despondent; she stayed with, indeed clung to the other women, but she had little to say. I put it down to her being recently ill. Once I saw

Adam approach her, looking hang dog, but she turned quickly away from him and came to help me peel the potatoes. I wondered momentarily about it, but I was all too conscious that married couples were under a strain in the hospital environment, and I did not think a spat between Sally and Adam worth worrying about.

After dinner the men built a huge fire in the old fieldstone fireplace and we crowded about it, some of us sitting in the settle on one side of the hearth. Charlie produced hymnals and suggested we sing the Whittier hymn, "O Lord and Father of Mankind." Several of the men had good bass voices and Sally a lovely contralto; we were so pleased with the sounds we were making we went on to sing our old favorites including, "That Cause Will Never Be Lost Nor Stayed."

When we had exhausted our repertory, and the fire was beginning to burn low, it seemed natural to settle into a silence. I was still new to Quaker meeting, although Allen and I occasionally attended one in Baltimore, and often had trouble quieting down my thoughts and opening myself to the silence.

Tonight however the silence seemed different, alive; I could feel my friends about me, sense their presence and their very being in a way that wasn't possible when we were talking. In the silence there was no need to make an impression on them, or defend myself against their imagined criticism, I could in fact relax with them into a deeper level of being.

Sam broke the silence, to my great surprise. He who would never permit a serious word to be said, who turned every thought into a mockery of itself, who said he had turned his back on religion and philosophy, was scarcely the voice one would have expected to hear. Yet he spoke simply but well, of the very thing I had been feeling, a sense of oneness. The universe was to him, he said, a series of concentric circles, each encompassing the other, until one was down to the self. Here in this room we had the best-sized circle for individual growth and development.

We were quiet after he stopped speaking, watching the little blue flames run up and down the glowing logs, and the occasional

coals chink into the ashes. Then Charlie spoke, more conven-
tionally I thought, but well, about the resource of human companionship to strengthen us all when we were facing frustrations
such as CPS exposed us to. He was, he said, grateful for the rest of
us for being his friends, and helping him to know there was more
than one way to worship God.

Were we really worshiping here, I wondered. My mind began
to race down a familiar corridor. With self deception all about
us at Sykesville, how much were we deceiving ourselves? To my
surprise and shock I suddenly heard myself speaking the words
aloud, asking what we really had to believe in, how indeed could
we find anything to believe in, when each day opened at our
feet new chasms of human depravity? Was it possible to go on
believing anyway, to believe against belief, because the world
needed faith so badly? Was this what the world of today demanded
of us? Was I condemned to live always with an inquiring mind but
a believing heart?

When I stopped my face was hot with embarrassment. This
was not the sort of thing the others wanted to hear. My need to
speak was compulsive, not inspired. But Allen, sitting next to me,
reached over and squeezed my hand, and the quiet, when it came
again, had that same living quality, a supportiveness, a tender-
ness, that made me feel my outburst was accepted. In fact perhaps
I had voiced a strand in our common experience.

The silence deepened and lasted a long time. I felt better for
what I had said, and relaxed into it. Could it be, I mused, that
there were good surprises as well as bad surprises to be experienced? Maybe there were fountains, as well as chasms, within the
human heart. I felt, I realized, like a swimmer who had been struggling against the undertow until she had grown tired and a little
frightened. Suddenly, as she nears the breakers a wave lifts her,
and carries her forward, and then another, and another. But whence
came the uplifting wave in my spirit? It seemed to be something
within me and my friends, and yet coming from beyond. That
sense of a deep mysterious force at the base of my being, which I
experienced under the stars, or in the middle of a lake, or in the

apple orchard near Sykesville, came through powerfully here among my friends. It felt tonight as though new life of the spirit was thrusting up in me through the dead leaves of the past.

Quaker style, we ended our silence with the clasping of hands. I felt moved and, as the old Friends used to say, tendered by the silence. I wanted to clasp hands with all my friends, to assure them that there was warmth in me too, beneath the surface of the old sharp-tongued, critical Marge. I wanted particularly to speak to Sally, who seemed so troubled, to tell her I was her friend, to ask if I could help. But I didn't speak and we gradually put the fireside mood away from ourselves; there was joking and a general move toward the kitchen for cider and donuts.

In the morning it had cleared a little, and we took a wet walk around the farmyard, noting buds on the lilac and forsythia, and finding to our delight a small bunch of crocuses huddled on the south side of the house by the rain barrel. Down near the creek skunk cabbages were unfolding and the first yellow blooms of lesser celandine appearing. On the lawn, a robin hopped. A craggy and neglected apple tree held fat buds against the pearly sky. Everywhere there was a trickling, a dripping, a stirring of early spring. Soon it became darker and began to rain again, but the walk had raised our spirits.

Lunch was our last meal at the farmhouse. We were in no particular hurry to get back to the hospital, but we had promised to be out by 3 p.m. and we did not know whether or not another group was coming into the farmhouse hard on our heels. Having paid nothing for the weekend, we thought the least we could do was to give the place a good cleaning, so after our meal we fell to. One thing to be said of mental hospital experience was that we all, male and female alike, became expert with a mop or a broom as well as truly distinguished with a waxer. With the educated talents of all of us at work we had the place gleaming before we left.

The off and on weather had lightened after lunch but darkened again when we were ready to leave and the first tentative drops of a soft spring rain were falling as we climbed into the old chevy. We were to return to the hospital in two carloads; our amiable friend Jim ferrying first Allen, myself, Sally and Adam, and on the second trip, the Platts and the Durdens. Whether it was the dismal afternoon, or our own fatigue I did not know, but we said little on the way back. Jim, always sociable, made several attempts at conversation, but I was wrapped in my own thoughts and Adam and Sally were silent.

"Well, back to the old grind," Allen said as we pulled up to the attendants' group at the Men's Colony, where Adam and Sally lived. "See you on the ward bright and early, Adam."

"O, didn't I tell you?" Adam asked. "I won't be in 'till noon, Sally is going home to visit her parents and I'm putting her on the train first thing in the morning."

"You are?" I asked Sally, gaping foolishly. My work brought me into contact with Sally's office on a regular basis, and I felt fairly sure no one there had heard about any such plan. "Is something the matter at home?"

"I wrote the office a little note," Sally said. "I hope they won't have too much trouble getting along without me for a bit."

"You aren't going to be gone long?" I asked.

Sally and Adam were busy climbing out of the car and getting their luggage and did not respond. I looked from one to the other, then to Allen, and then back, but there seemed to be no clue. "Well, have a good time and hurry back," I said lamely, as Jim shifted gears and prepared to return for the second ferry load.

When we were alone in our room Allen commented that he had noticed that Adam was not acting like himself all the past week. "I think they're having some problem with their marriage," he surmised. "I suspect we weren't too well advised to insist on their coming on the weekend with us."

"We didn't insist," I objected, and then I realized that I had. When Sally had raised objections I had overridden them with my enthusiasm. They must come. We were going to have such a good time. It wouldn't be complete without them. Why couldn't I ever learn to listen to people?

"Gosh, that kind of ruins the weekend for me," I confided to Allen. "I felt so good about it and about us all last night."

"You never know quite what is going on in other people's lives," Allen remarked. "I guess the best you can do is let them be, and offer them whatever support you have to give."

I looked at him admiringly. He sometimes seemed so much wiser than I, and so much more attentive to other people. I was so often engrossed in my own feelings, whether guilt or enthusiasm, doubt or faith, that I became unaware, as in this case, of how I might be affecting others.

"Well, marriages have their ups and downs," I said tritely. We smiled at each other. Our marriage seemed at the moment on its way up. We were knitting closer together, putting the tiger's milk episode behind us, and it was good to be alone, after the busy weekend, with the soft spring rain washing at our window and the long spring evening ahead.

The week after our retreat, spring came to Sykesville full tilt. The forsythia frothed with yellow bloom, the maples were in bright red bud, violets twinkled throughout the grass. In the distance, the woods were pink with rising sap, and the willows along the creek turned bright yellow.

The return of spring marked the end of my first year at Sykesville as well as my twenty-fourth year of life. I could not help looking back with some satisfaction over the progress I had made. The present me, white-coated, assured, accepted as part of the inner group that ran the big hospital, was a far cry from the scared and conflicted greenhorn I had been on arrival. I could turn the heavy key in the lock and walk on the violent ward now without even a ghost of my former fears.

The 12th of April was a lovely day, warmer than any so far. I had appointments all morning, and spent the afternoon writing up my interviews. At 5 p.m. my day's work was over, but as usual I stayed in my office, writing a letter home to my parents, and had an early supper with Allen in the attendants' dining room. I was just returning from this meal when I saw the head nurse standing in the middle of the hall. She looked at me strangely.

"Mrs. Bacon, have you heard the news?" she asked.

"What news?" I inquired.

"It's Roosevelt," she said. "The president is dead."

I stared at her, shocked and unbelieving.

"O no," I said. "It can't be."

"The news just came over the radio," she confirmed. "He died this afternoon in Georgia."

"It's hard to take in," I said.

"When I first heard it I didn't believe it," Mrs. Jenkins affirmed. She continued to look at me oddly, and I realized that despite her own shock she was curious to see how I would react. After all, I had opposed Roosevelt's war. Did I deserve to share in his mourning?

"Did they say what he died of?" I asked

"I think it was a cerebral hemorrhage," she replied. "There's a group down in the attendants' lounge listening to the radio if you want more news."

"Thanks, perhaps I'll go there," I said. In fact, the attendants' lounge was tacitly regarded as off limits to the c.o.s and their wives. I realized Mrs. Jenkins was deliberately ignoring this prohibition and inviting me to go there in a burst of griefborn generosity, but I didn't really want to go. I felt an urgent need to be with my own kind, and as soon as Mrs. Jenkins turned away I started down the stairs, almost automatically for Ralph's office. Then I remembered that he was on vacation, having announced rather suddenly that he was tired and needed to get away.

Instead, I climbed back upstairs and stood in the middle of the wide front hall, deliberating. It was almost two hours until Allen came off the ward. I couldn't go back to my office and try to work; my need to talk to someone was too great. I finally decided to walk over to the attendants' quarters and see if anyone from the unit was in the basement recreation room.

As if to deny the sad news, the sky was suffused with the pink of sunset, and the air sweet and soft. It was an evening for lovers, not mourners. I walked quickly across the grounds, my hands clenched. I had been a child of twelve when Franklin Roosevelt was elected; all my years of adolescence and early adulthood he had been in the White House. He seemed a fixture, like a father. Sometimes, like a father, he made me angry but more often, in the past twelve years

I had been on his side. I remembered well the steely glint of the sun striking the roofs of Hooverville along the Hudson, and my own dismay at my artist father's not being able to find work. I had been grateful for the New Deal, and angry at its critics.

He had gotten us into this war, some of our fellow pacifists said. Yes, but I still could not believe that he had connived and plotted to get us into the war, as some people were beginning to hint. Granted his assumptions were not those of Gandhi, what else was there for him to do? Even Gandhi had said that it was necessary to oppose evil, if one could not use nonviolent means then one must use violent ones. Besides, only a tiny minority of people even discussed nonviolence as a remote possibility. When times changed, when the majority came to the conviction that war was futile, then it would be time to have a pacifist in the White House.

In the recreation room of the Attendant's Quarters I found several of our friends, including Jim and Alice, huddled around the radio. CBS was broadcasting live coverage of reaction to the news from passersby in New York and Washington, and from correspondents at Hot Springs. Grief and shock as well as pathos came through in every interview. I noticed that Alice's eyes were red, and that she held a wadded up kleenex in one hand.

After we had listened for a bit, Jim got up, sighed, and walked away, pounding his fist into the palm of the other hand. His place was taken by another of the men, and so it went for an hour or more, unit members drifting in and out to share the news. Little was said. What was there to say? We shared a wordless depression. We had cut ourselves off from the world, hoping, intending to make our lives into a pattern for what the real world might become. But in fact we had achieved little, and now the war we had opposed was all but over and the leader we had turned from was gone.

Sam and Allen had heard the news on the ward. They came over shortly after eight, and we four sat in the Durden's room drinking coffee, smoking cigarettes while we fretfully flicked the dials for more news.

"Well, were we right or were we wrong?" Sam finally asked, grinding out a butt in a thick hospital saucer.

"We'll have to wait for history to answer that question," Allen said. "Who was it that said, 'you become what you hate?' If we're right we'll be as militaristic as Germany in another twenty- five years. And as surrounded by enemies. And as repressive within. It's not a happy position, needing disaster for vindication."

"Then I hope we were wrong," Alice said passionately. " Who wants to bring children into such a world."

I knew the Burdens were beginning to think about having a family. We were, too but it was impossible to make plans until the war finally ended. Now the death of Roosevelt reminded us how uncertain was life. We said good night and went back to our own room to bed.

That was Thursday. We had the weekend to recover and regain some sort of even keel. Then a fresh blow fell and rocked our little world completely.

I heard about it in almost the same way. I was hurrying down the corridor toward the lunchroom for breakfast when I ran into Janet, and saw that she had been crying.

"What's the matter?" I asked.

"O Marge, haven't you heard?" she asked. "it's so awful but I guess its really got to be true. I just would never have believed . . . of all people. . . ."

"What happened?" I asked, bewildered.

"O Marge, it's Ralph. Ralph has left the unit. He and Sally are together. Sally is going to get a divorce and marry Ralph."

"Not Ralph," I said stupidly. "He wouldn't . . . he couldn't."
"That's just it," Janet said, "But unfortunately he did."

Slowly we learned the details. Ralph had notified the Brethren and Selected Service of his desire to resign and to be moved to a different unit weeks ago. Now he was on his way to California. Sally was with him, planning to stop off at Reno. Adam had gone to Kansas City, leaving a few days ago. No one knew what his plans were.

The news spread by word of mouth throughout the hospital. One could tell immediately who had learned it. Members of the unit looked lost, shattered, stunned; the regular attendants were brimming with glee. So much for the conchies and their claim to moral superiority. Even Matilda seemed to be taking malicious satisfaction from the news; licking her lips like a greedy cat, hungry for more details.

I gave her little satisfaction, but alone with Allen and Alice and Sam I felt almost obsessed with the need to keep talking about it, going over and over the clues we had seen and missed. We remembered different things; I, the day I ran into Ralph's office and came upon them talking so earnestly; Alice, the rumor that once floated through the hospital that Ralph was in love with a c.o.'s wife; Allen, the gradual change he had seen in Adam. It was as though we were all scrabbling hungrily over the past for a sign of what we should have known, might have done.

The elopement was devastating to all of us. For me it intensified the struggle I had been having to accept the concept of the potential goodness in human nature—the "that of God in everyone" of which the Quakers spoke. If even Ralph and Sally, who seemed to represent the very best qualities of our unit, had felt it necessary to deceive Adam and the rest of us, what hope indeed was there for building a better and a warless world?

Allen did not share my sense of the connection between personal action and political theory, and it began to become clear to me that my questioning jeopardized our future. Maybe I really wasn't cut out for a lifetime of idealism. Perhaps I wasn't a good enough person to be Allen's wife. In my marriage, as well as in the life we would lead together, I would always be trying to be a better person than I felt I was, always trying to live up to some impossible ideal. The prospect of years and years of this ahead made me suddenly very tired.

It was a strange spring; the days full of blossom and birdsong following one another while we struggled with desolation and guilt. The news of advancing American troops in Germany indicated the war would soon be over but with Roosevelt gone, with our unit in turmoil, the sudden probability that we would be released within the next year did not seem real.

The Brethren Service Committee decided to select someone from the unit to carry on in Ralph's job until a more permanent replacement could be found. Various names were suggested, but in the end it came down to two: Jim Hargreaves, a big, friendly Brethren farmer, and Allen. I was proud of Allen and sure that he would be elected, but I had the feeling that this recognition was coming a little late.

Of all the state employees to take the news of Ralph and Sally's elopement as a sign of vindication, the most emphatic was my non-speaking secretary. She could not quite bring herself to break the silence, even to crow, but she managed to let me know how she felt, whispering and giggling with the other secretaries whenever I entered the central office, banging my cylinders down in front of me in a cross manner, making the most of my mistakes. With Sally herself across the hall to console me, I had been equal to all this before, but now I couldn't take it any more, and lurked in my office until I was sure no one was around before putting my nightly offering of dictation on her desk.

V.E. Day, the 5th of May came, and with it wild rejoicing from which we stayed aloof. Word was beginning to come back about Dachau and Buchenwald. It was hard to think of those remaining emaciated men and women longing for deliverance, and to know that we had chosen not to be among those who had been on their way to rescue them. I felt an ever deepening guilt about it. Allen pointed out that the conditions that produced Dachau had been in place before we were born, and that we could not take responsibility for all evil in the world. Our own country had been negligent in helping Jews escape from Hitler. We had never even accepted our quota of German citizens during that period, and we had turned back a shipload of refugees who sought haven on our shores. When the head of the American Friends Service Committee had offered to provide at private expense German speaking volunteers at every consular office in Germany in order to expedite emigration to the United States, he had been told to mind his own business. There were many ways that the world could have intervened long before the concentration camps began their policy of final solution. Pacifist opinion had been overlooked at the time of Versailles, at the 1930 World Disarmanent Conference, the failure of which triggered the rise of Hitler, at every step of the way. We could not now be expected to feel responsible for the results. We could not go over the past, but we could look forward. It was now up to us to prove that we could build a world in which such horrors could never happen again.

The unit election was held the following Tuesday, May 8. After a unit business meeting, conducted by the assistant director, we all placed our written ballots in a box and went to our rooms, leaving a committee to add up the results. I looked forward to Allen's being unit director; he would keep the same office hours as I did in the admissions unit, and we could visit together off and on during the day, just as I used to visit with Ralph. I said something about these hopes to Sam.

"Don't forget, Marge, this group leans heavily toward country men," Sam cautioned. "Allen is not from the country."

"But they all like him," I argued. "They all respect him."

"Yes, but he's a college man, and some of them envy him," Sam reminded me.

We were eating breakfast with Alice and Sam the next morning when Jim, looking hang dog, came to our table with the news. Hargreaves had won the election. Allen smiled philosophically and said he thought it was a good choice. From now on the major problem would be arranging discharges for the men and helping them make plans for college or for jobs. It meant dealing extensively with the Brethren Service Committee and Jim was a good Brethren. I said nothing, but felt angry and bitterly betrayed. Why didn't Allen fight for things like this, I thought? Was it really strong to accept defeat so gracefully?

The spring continued to be a time of change. Soon after V.E. day, the c.o.s who had been in CPS from the beginning began to be discharged. Allen who had been drafted in 1943 still had almost a year to go, but it looked as though Sam would be out in the fall, and Charlie soon thereafter. As the weeks passed we all began to plan for the hazy future toward which we had been moving so long.

For most members of the unit, the planning was easy. They would go back and pick up their lives where they had been interrupted by the draft; become again farmers, or teachers, or auto mechanics, or ministers or plumbers, as they had previously been. A few of the college graduates had decided on the basis of the Sykesville years to go into psychology or psychiatry or social work. Many of the married couples were beginning to plan their families. We talked about how we could raise infants free of guilt and hidden rage. Perhaps out of this experience we could bring up a generation that would be able to free the world of war.

Allen struggled with his plans. He went to Philadelphia to talk with the AFSC about reconstruction work in postwar Europe, but they told him they were not going to be able to use the large numbers they had sent to Europe at the end of World War I. Then they had been almost alone in the field of reconstruction; now there were other relief organizations and government agencies in the field. They were going to do specialized work, and needed people already experienced in refugee resettlement.

He then thought about going on with his interest in consumer cooperatives. But the movement seemed to be losing steam in the United States. It had never caught on in working-class neighborhoods, and the middle-class liberals who had been its main support seemed to be drawing away, unwilling to spend the time on countless meetings it took to keep a co-op going.

Instead, he decided to go to graduate school to prepare himself to teach, and ultimately for educational administration. Becoming headmaster of a new, experimental school, where one could find ways of exciting students about the social issues of the day, seemed to him at the time the best possible way to start building a new world. There was a special Quaker scholarship fund he could apply for, and Harvard School of Education looked like a good place to go.

"I don't want you to feel that you have to support me, Marge," he explained. "You gave up a lot to come here. I want you to do what you most want, whether it's writing or having a baby."

We had begun to think about having a baby, just like the others. And yet lingering doubts about whether I was going to make a good wife for Allen persisted. I turned away to hide the tears.

In June the Durdens and we spent a two week vacation in the Pocono Mountain cottage which was owned by one of Allen's aunts. Two of Allen's cousins, one with two babies, were there also. We played tennis on the clay courts, canoed on the lake, swam, picnicked, climbed a mountain, played cards every night, took time out to see the stars. It was a time of rest and healing, a time to begin turning our faces away from the past and toward the future. We both enjoyed little Stuart and Mary. Several months later Alice announced happily that she was pregnant, and the baby had probably been conceived in the Poconos. It made a special bond.

Despite the idyllic interlude in the Poconos it had been a strange spring and it was a strange summer. The war in Asia dragged on and on; half the world was rejoicing and beginning a new life while in the other half the killing continued. Alice began to knit baby clothes and talk about the future. I envied her, but I didn't understand how she could have such faith. There had been too many bad surprises. Was another one possible? It was. On August 6 we heard that an atomic bomb had been dropped on Hiroshima and Nagasaki, and our world would never be safe again.

Chapter IX

Dr. Wiseman was leaving. He had bought his own shock box, and was setting up practice as a private psychiatrist in the city. It was rumored that he had taken advantage of his position at the hospital to recruit his first lot of patients; discharged men and women were invited to continue treatments with him on a private basis.

"I don't know why you feel upset about this," Allen said. "It's quite in character."

"Yes, but it seems like such a ruthless thing to do," I said. Actually it was the fact that he was deserting us that seemed ruthless. Sykesville had been, in a curious way, a sort of ark on which we all—c.o.s and state employees, refugee doctors and patients—rode out the storm. Now the storm was over, the gangplank was down, and the passengers were leaving. I think I might have felt a sense of loss, just then, if my ever-silent secretary had departed. One could become accustomed even to those who hated you, I discovered, and it was easy to grow to depend upon the accustomed, even more than the beloved.

I had even grown to like Dr. Wiseman, despite my disapproval of his ethics. During our office chats he had told me that he once wanted to be a writer, and he was very interested in reading some of my pieces, although his criticisms were all wrong; he wanted me to be more baroque just when I was learning to be simple.

Dr. Wiseman and Matilda had always been at swords point, since her theories about the therapeutic role of social work had no part in his mechanical, save-them-by-shock rationale. (She rationalized shock treatments, too, but in a much more elaborate style.) I was rather surprised therefore when she defended him vigorously at our next conference.

"You're so critical of us all, Marge, these days. I wonder if there is something you are projecting," she hazarded.

I started to answer back hotly, then thought better of it. It seemed to me lately that Matilda was trying to invade my privacy, find some sort of vicarious satisfaction from the struggle I was waging within myself. She was a lonely woman, I had come to realize, and it was natural for her to want to become involved in the lives of her workers. Previously I had felt that involvement was innocent, and for my benefit. Now I was not so sure. At any rate, I had too much to sort out to let my guard down, just then, or to her.

"It's an uneasy time," I said, fending her off. "None of us knows exactly when we are going to be leaving, nor where we are going. I suppose actually a lot of the other doctors will be going too."

It was a mean remark. Matilda, too, must have felt herself on an emptying ark. The difference was that I could and would eventually go too; she was left chained by her family situation to a lifetime here.

"Yes, change is very difficult for us all," Matilda said sighing. "Actually we grow through change, but we resist it, clinging to little islands of adjustment and refusing to launch forth into new adventures. Then when we decide to change, we must reject the old in order to give us strength to go on to the new. I wonder if that is what you are in the midst of, Marge?"

"Perhaps," I said. This was a standard element in her philosophy, and one I had heard often before. Patients had to reject the hospital in order to move back into the real world; patients had to reject the real world in order to adjust to the treatment situation; departing social workers had to reject her in order to get ready for the break. In relation to myself, however, it sounded fresh, and plausible. The question was, which world was I rejecting?

She smiled, but rather bleakly, I thought. "I hope we can see more of you and Allen before you go," she said. "Do you know for sure when that is going to be?"

"Probably at Christmas time," I told her. Allen's discharge wasn't due until next May, but shortly after the unit election, the Brethren Service Committee had asked him to become the director of another camp in Maryland for the duration of CPS. Probably the election itself had brought him to their attention. From my point of view he was receiving the recognition he deserved too little and too late, but at least we were getting away from Sykesville.

I rose to go, my hour being up. Matilda followed Otto Rank in believing in the strict use of time. Somehow my glance strayed across her desk, and I saw she had a new copy of the *Journal of Social Work* in a pile before her and the title of the lead article checked in red. Matilda saw my glance, stood up, and abruptly pushed some papers across her desk to cover the magazine. To my surprise, she flushed.

I expected her to explain her reaction, but she said nothing, and since there was nothing for me to say the silence lengthened. "Well, I must be off," I finally said lamely. "Until next week then."

"Until this time next week," Matilda said, repeating mechanically.

Still mystified, I left her office and paused in the hall outside. Her secretary, who usually sat at the reception desk, was momentarily out of the room. I glanced across her desk, and saw a small stack of the *Journal of Social Work* with that same check mark. On impulse I picked up one copy, slipped it into my knitting bag, and took it to the admissions office.

Unfortunately, there was no chance to look at it. Sitting in the anteroom of my office were two police officers, holding between them a tousled, distraught looking young woman who twisted and turned in their grasp. There was something vaguely familiar about her. I looked again and saw that she was a patient of Dr. Wiseman's, discharged a few months ago.

I called the central office and asked them to bring me Deborah Levy's file. I then called Dr. Wiseman. "It's Debby," I told him. "She's back, and she seems very disturbed."

The police officers let go of Debby and she came slowly into my office looking around suspiciously.

"Please sit down," I ventured.

"Where is he?" Debby wanted to know. "Where is that motherfucker? Are you his wife?"

Dr. Wiseman came striding in at this point. Instantly Debby was galvanized by hatred. She began to hiss like a snake, and to writhe her body in a derisive satire of sex. "I know what it is you want, Wisey, old boy, just one thing, just the same old thing," she said, spitting the words out. She slid down to the floor and began to pull up her skirt.

"Get up now, Debby, and act like a good girl," Dr. Wiseman said.

"You better get down here, Wisey," Debby answered, writhing and spitting. "Like you used to do before."

Dr. Wiseman shrugged and rang for the attendants. We sat waiting for them, frozen into our positions like players in a game of statues; me shrinking at my desk, Dr. Wiseman looking expansive and satisfied with himself at the large desk, Debby still on the floor, unbuttoning her blouse. Was her accusation possible, I suddenly wondered. She had a beautiful body. Or was this thought totally unworthy of me? I seemed to be becoming distrustful of everyone. It was a great relief when the attendants from South II-A came, and took her away.

"Poor Debby," I remarked, as soon as they had taken her away. "She seemed so confident when she left."

"O well," Dr. Wiseman said. "A few shock treatments and she'll likely be herself again."

"But how long will that last?" I asked

"She may need it again and again," he said easily. "Some people take insulin all their lives, you know. I may be able to arrange to treat her in the city."

I thought I could see the dollar signs shining in his eyes. And what else? I said nothing and turned slightly away. He stopped to pat my shoulder on the way toward the door. "You take life much too seriously, Marge. You want to right everything. It can't be done, my dear. Sooner or later you'll come to see that, and maybe you'll be better friends with yourself. We're all human, you know."

"Thanks," I said, touched despite myself by the kindness of his remarks, and feeling guilty for my suspicions. I sighed, wrote a brief paragraph on the admission, took the file back to the central office, and then remembered the magazine in my knitting bag. I pulled it out and read the table of contents. "The Locus and Function of a Psychiatric Social Worker in a State Hospital," the first article was titled, and next to it, the name of the author, Matilda Van Dusen, MSW.

I stared blankly. Somehow my article had gotten into this Journal by mistake and been published. And somehow, Matilda's name had been incorrectly attached to it. I was ready to run down to her office and show her the enormous error, when I looked again and saw the check mark in her hand. Blood rushed to my cheeks. This was no accident. Matilda's famous inability to write, her longing to be published, her guilty reaction this afternoon when I saw the Journal on her desk. All the pieces fitted together. In the language of the c.o.s, I had been volunteered.

Suddenly I felt as though I would suffocate if I didn't get out of my tight little office. I looked at the clock. It was almost four; unlikely that any more admissions would come that day. And if they came, who cared? It was time to get over being so "duty happy" as the c.o.s said. It was time to break down. I picked up my pocketbook and my knitting bag and walked across the hall and down the long stairs to open air and freedom.

It was a glorious September afternoon. The sky was a bowl of clearest blue without a cloud in sight, a warm sun beat down and a golden haze shimmered over the far away meadows. Here and there the first sharp colors of swamp maple and golden elm touched the woods. The air seemed still—one could hear the far off cawing of crows, and the husky voices of a few disturbed patients shouting from the hill.

I walked down the path, hesitated at the road, then decided to hike over the hill to our favorite apple orchard. It was time as a matter of fact for the apples to be ripe again. "Sunburst and stubble thrust, this moment of togetherness." I remember the poem

I had written at this time last year. The memory brought an etching of pain to the back of my mouth.

I walked quickly over the hill, hardly taking time to watch where my feet were going. I felt very angry, but whether at Matilda, or Dr. Wiseman, or Ralph and Sally, or the unit, or Allen, or Sykesville, or myself, I wasn't quite sure. I was betrayed, but was I myself the betrayer? I had learned in this last year to look inward for answers; I wondered if it were every going to be possible to place my anger entirely outside myself.

The orchard was as I had remembered it, warm and fragrant with rotting drops. Here and there wasps hovered over the sweet brown carcasses of fallen apples. I found a place to sit where I could look out across the rolling meadows, and sank down wearily. Ralph had been with us this time last year, I remembered. It seemed like five years ago, a time of lost innocence.

Above me, a hawk circled, hung motionless, mounted as he caught the updraft. I watched him idly for a while. His effortlessness reminded me of swimming, of being lifted toward shore by a wave. It would be so good to feel that you didn't have to do it all for yourself, that there was something, never mind what name you gave it, on which to rely, to rest, to rise with. If I knew how to do it, I thought, I would pray. Or worship, as the Quakers did, in silence. But I was still a neophyte. If praying was swimming, I had not even learned to dog paddle.

And what was I to pray for? A sign, I thought, a sign. I knew now that I simply could not go on with this life I had chosen, a life based on the premise that humans could learn to live with one another in peace, until I began to have a little faith in the good inherent in the human race, and in myself as well. The Quaker belief in that of God in everyone seemed to bring out the best in people. I saw that operating with Allen. I kept seeing only the worst in myself and in others, and like a self-fulfilling prophecy, I kept experiencing the betrayals I expected.

Perhaps I was overstating the case. After all, Ralph and Sally had run away, Matilda had plagiarized my article, Wiseman had been ruthless. There was evil in human nature. What would have happened if Gandhi had confronted Hitler? Gandhi claimed that the very principle of civil disobedience alone would have prevailed upon the conscience of the good Germans to turn away from the madman, and withdraw their cooperation from the system, but it was a little hard to visualize at times. You really could never know for sure, either way. You had to base your faith on a leap into the dark. But to make the leap, you had to have faith. Not that goodness would always prevail, but that there was always potential. Allen could dismiss occasional failings as human, while keeping his belief that on balance the good would overcome the evil. I badly wanted to believe this, too, but right now it would be good to have some confirmation, some sign to cling to.

If I were going to turn aside from my commitment to pacifism, I wasn't sure that I could go on being married to Allen, trying to accept and fit myself to Quakerism. If I were going to call all this into question now would be the time to do so. Allen would be discharged in the spring and go on to graduate school. We had been thinking about having a child, but I was not pregnant. This would be the logical juncture to part and each go his or her own way. It would be painful, but less so than at any other time, perhaps.

Ours wasn't going to be an easy marriage. We felt and saw things differently; often we did not understand each other's reactions. Allen used to joke about his halo, and ask me if I thought it needed shining, but in fact because of his Quaker upbringing, to subdue anger and submerge his interests in that of the group seemed natural to him. I thought of it at the time as goodness, and felt myself critical and angry and selfish in contrast. It would be nice to escape that feeling.

And yet, and yet. Were marriages always supposed to be easy? I was beginning to learn, as Matilda had been teaching me, that growth was always painful but always necessary. If you didn't grow, you died. Maybe growth and struggle were as necessary in a marriage as in life. Anyway, I loved Allen. There was that fact, I really loved him. I couldn't imagine going off and leaving him now.

And about this life that I seemed to have chosen by marrying a Quaker. Was it really true that one had to have faith in order to live it? Did Allen indeed have such faith? Even if I left him, would I be able to settle for a life with no built-in aspirations for a better world? Even if you were self deceiving, naive, a do- gooder; all the things of which we were accused, was there a better set of assumptions on which to build your life?

I had been childish, I thought. Childish to fall into this depression. Childish to demand a sign. There was no sign. The sign had to come from within. To be adult was to go on, having faith without demanding proof. Being able to move into the unknown without this everlasting questioning of mine.

The sun was beginning to set across the woods. I suddenly discovered that I was cold and cramped. I got up and started back towards the hospital. It must be practically dinner time. Probably Allen was looking for me. If I were going to be mature I would have to stop this way of running off to be alone.

In the front hall I ran into an attendant's wife. She gave me a rather odd look. "Guess what?" she said. "I've just been talking with a friend of yours."

"A friend of mine?"

"Yes, Agnes Holler."

"You've been talking to Agnes?" I repeated, feeling stupid. "Agnes hasn't talked to anyone in years."

"Yes, Agnes," Florence said. "This was the day she was scheduled for a lobotomy. They were shorthanded and they asked me to help. I was there when they operated. And, you know, it worked. For the first time in twenty-two years she talked coherently. And Marge, you know whom she talked about? You. She asked where you were and how you were. She said, 'How is that nice Mrs. Bacon. She is the only friend I've had since I came to this place.' It seems like a miracle, doesn't it?"

I continued to stare at Florence while wave after wave of reaction swept over me. The love I had felt for Agnes because she had helped me overcome my fear. Perfect love had cast out fear instead of the reverse. I hadn't really known before that, imperfect as I was, I could be the channel of such love. And the fact that that love had found its way through all the barriers of Agnes' madness and isolation to the essential miraculous person inside.

"Yes, I said slowly, "like a miracle, a sign." The wave lifted me again, and carried me forward. I began to cry.

Epilogue

I went to see Agnes Holler a few days later, but already she had reverted to her former state, and was muttering over her trousseau, "and little yellow napkins with pink embroidery, and little green tea towels." I held her hand and talked with her, and she was gentle with me, but absent, just as she had been before. She was considerably thinner and sicker than she had been when I first encountered her; it seemed likely that she would soon die. I checked her records once more, but there seemed to be no way of contacting any family member to keep in touch with her. When I said goodbye I knew it was for the last time.

We left Sykesville shortly after this. Allen was asked to be director of a CPS camp at the Patuxent Wildlife Refugee in Bowie, Maryland. I was pregnant with my first child, and lived and worked in nearby Washington, D. C. Here our daughter Peggy was born. As an adult, she became interested in mental health, and is now a practicing clinical psychologist. One of her early jobs was helping to place patients from a state mental hospital back in the community.

Allen and I have had a long and adventurous life. But Agnes has stayed with me, as a symbol of the power of love to overcome violence, and of a power both within myself and beyond, flowing through me at times powerfully, at times sluggishly, but at bedrock, always there. At times of crisis, at times when I lose faith in the goodness of people, at times when the cause seems hopeless, I remember Agnes and I begin to believe again.

Love is the Hardest Lesson

was composed on a Power MacIntosh 7600 computer using Adobe Pagemaker 6.0 and typefaces from the Adobe Type Library: Goudy for the text, and Caslon for the cover.

1500 copies were printed in the United States by Thomson-Shore, Inc., Dexter, Michigan in November 1999. It was printed on 60# Gladfelter Recycled paper.

History of the Typefaces

In 1915 Frederick Goudy designed Goudy Old Style, his twenty-fifth typeface and his first for American Type-founders. One of the most popular typefaces ever produced, it distinctive features include diamond-shaped dots on the i, the j, and punctuation marks; the upturned ear of the g, and the base of the e and the l. In 1925, Frederick Goudy designed heavy versions of Goudy Old Style. Their huge success led to the addition of several other weights. In subsequent years, American typefounders created additions to the family.

William Caslon released his first typefaces in 1722. They were based on seventeenth-century Dutch old style designs, then used extensively in England. Because of their incredible practicality, Caslon's designs met with instant success. Caslon's type became popular throughout Europe and the American colonies: printer Benjamin Franklin hardly used any other typefaces. The first printings of the American Declaration of Independence and the Constitution were set in Caslon. Adobe's Caslon was designed by Carol Twombly who studied specimen pages printed by William Caslon between 1734 and 1770.

Book Design by
Eva Fernandez Beehler and Rebecca Kratz Mays